D0191416

SWEDEN

An Illustrated History

Illustrated Histories from Hippocrene

SWEDEN
An Illustrated History

Martina Sprague

Hippocrene Books, Inc.
New York

© 2005 Martina Sprague

All Rights Reserved.

For information address:
  Hippocrene Books, Inc.
  171 Madison Avenue
  New York, NY 10016
  www.hippocrenebooks.com

Book design and composition by Susan A. Ahlquist, East Hampton, NY.

Cataloging in Publication data available from the Library of Congress.

ISBN 0-7818-1114-7

Printed in the United States of America.

Dedication

To Sylvia and Sören Lax,
my mother and father,
my two points of pride.

Acknowledgements

I would like to express my appreciation to the following museums in Sweden for granting me permission to photograph on-site:

Museum of History in Stockholm
Stockholm City Museum
The Vasa Museum
The Museum at Birka

Table of Contents

Preface

Sweden has a complex history. The country was first considered a national state in the era of King Gustav Vasa in the sixteenth century AD. Its borders changed regularly for many years after, and most of its recorded history occurred in what is the southern half of modern Sweden. In order to keep focused on the areas that were important to the time periods discussed, the events recorded here should be conceived in terms of people and happenings, rather than in terms of the modern geographical location of a city or town. Uppland (where Stockholm is located) is middle Sweden, everything north of Uppland is northern Sweden, and everything south of Uppland is southern Sweden. The northern half of modern Sweden, including the area of Norrland, is sparsely populated and is discussed only briefly.

Throughout history, and especially in the Middle Ages, the families of the rulers of the Nordic countries frequently intermarried and are too numerous to mention in a book this size. I have therefore chosen to discuss those who, in my opinion, were the most prominent in shaping Sweden into the nation it is today.

In order to convey the specific meaning and feel of those Swedish words or concepts that come up, I have written the Swedish word in *italics*, followed by a close translation within parenthesis. Many of the Swedish plural forms are irregular.

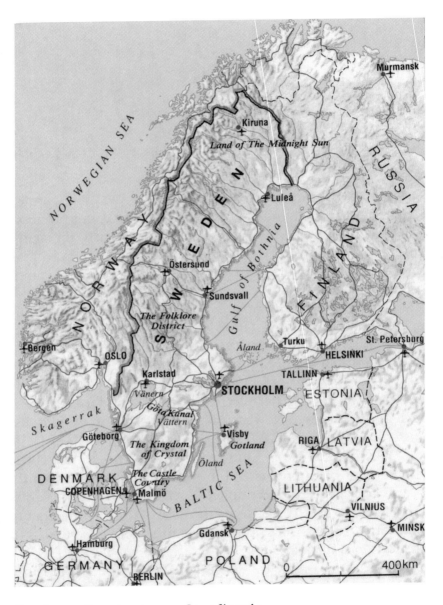

Sweden and contemporary Scandinavia.
Photo: www.imagebank.sweden.se © Stockholm Visitors Board.

For example, the word *storman* (upper class nobility), when put in its plural form, is *stormän*, while the word *frälse* (a privileged tax-exempt nobility) is the same in both its singular and plural form. For a brief education on Swedish letters and pronunciation, please refer to chapter 3, "Written Communication," and chapter 4, "Foreign Influence on Language."

Regarding important dates or time periods, I have specified all years as BC or AD for the first few chapters. However, for ease and clarity, once the narrative reaches the Middle Ages, all years are after the birth of Christ unless otherwise noted.

Most of the history of Sweden, from prehistoric times through its Middle Age, happened in the central and southern parts of modern Sweden, the shaded area on the map. Skåne, a region at modern Sweden's southern tip, has been subject to constant disputes and has fallen under Swedish or Danish ownership several times.

Introduction

The Swedish name for Sweden is Sverige and stems from Svea Rike, or the kingdom of the Svear. Prior to becoming Swedes, the people in Sweden were an amalgamation of folks called Svear, Östgötar, Västgötar, and Smålänningar, among others. Although Svealand (the areas around the lake Mälaren in the middle part of the country) and Götaland (in the more southern parts) didn't become a united Sweden until approximately the early Middle Ages, it is important to follow the thread of history that runs from the first settlers of the region, to the evolution of smaller communities, and to the industrialized Sweden that we know today.

As a child growing up and attending school in Sweden, I used to think history was boring but managed after some struggle to secure the equivalent of a B in my senior year. When I left, I felt I knew little, other than an endless memorization of years and names, about my Swedish heritage. So, why am I, twenty-five years later, writing a book about Swedish history?

Understanding history means understanding the people, the driving force behind our society. Neither kings nor generals but ordinary folks like you and I are the ones who shaped history and the events that led us to this day. With the exception of short visits to Sweden, my long absence has allowed me to gain perspective on and a deeper understanding of this country's evolution, including the people's beliefs and political system. History makes sense when you begin to see the correlations between events, and how they shape our future.

When my father and I rode the subway from the airport to his home during one of my recent visits to Sweden, I spoke loudly of my long trip and my excitement to be there. An elderly lady turned to me and commented that it wasn't necessary to let the world know who I was and where I had been. At first, I was offended by her remarks, but after mulling it over, I found it representative of the reserved Swedish mindset that has endured into the twenty-first century and is reflected in the Swedish national anthem: *Du gamla, du fria, du fjällhöga Nord, du tysta, du glädjenka sköna.* (Thou ancient, thou freeborn, thou mountainous north, thou quiet, thou joyful beauty.)

Swedish people feel that modesty is a virtue. In other words, you should be simple but not simplistic, you should have character but not be a character. Swedish people seldom express their emotions publicly. For example, you don't make small talk with a stranger on the subway, and you don't brag about yourself. If you ask for directions, you will get an answer, but if you want to talk about the weather or your family, you are not likely to get much response.

However, if you were to take the time and prod a little, you would find that the Swedes are proud of their country with its far-reaching nature, the quality of its healthcare and education, and particularly its democracy. For example, Sweden has the lowest child mortality rate in the world and ranks in the top percent among the world's nations in the quality of public education. The Social Democratic Party has held power by public election for the past sixty years (less two brief periods totaling nine years), and Sweden has the greatest political equality for women, with 149 (42.7 percent) of the 349 seats in the Swedish parliament held by women. The idea is that all people have equal value, regardless of their origin or status.

Modern Sweden is a constitutional monarchy, with the monarch acting as a ceremonial head of state. The Riksdag (parliament) is elected every four years and elects the prime minister. Sweden is perhaps best known for its long and strong democratic tradition, or as is written in Swedish law: *All offentlig makt i Sverige utår från folket* (All public power in Sweden emanates from the people).

To critics of Swedish socialism: Don't assume that the Swedes feel their political system is superior. Instead, question why, with all of the known weaknesses of socialism, the Swedes choose it with such consistency in free elections. Hopefully, this can be discovered through the study of history.

The first two chapters of this book describe briefly what we know about prehistoric times in the land that is now Sweden. The rest of the book explores in more depth the founding of Svea Rike, the wars and unions with what are now Denmark and Norway, the monarchs and dynasties, and the emergence of modern society. Rather than memorizing facts and time-lines, I encourage you to explore the correlation of events, the people's beliefs, and the social system that evolved throughout history. This comparison will help you gain a clearer view and understanding of the Swedish mindset as it relates to *det gamla landet* (the old country).

When I look at where we are today, I am amazed that a country formerly as barren and poor as Sweden was, where war, class structure, and oppression were often the norm, managed to rise and become one of the world's leaders in wealth, science, industry, and democracy.

Sweden Facts

Location: Approximately latitude 60 degrees north, lon-
            gitude 15 degrees east. Bordering Norway to the
            west and Finland to the east, separated from
            the bulk of Finland by the Baltic Sea to the east.

Size: Approximately 450,000 square kilometers,
            with a length to width ratio of approximately
            3 to 1.

Population: Approximately 9 million people. Average popu-
            lation density of 22 persons per square kilometer.
            Uneven distribution with 85 percent of the pop-
            ulation living in urban areas in southern and
            middle Sweden, and 15 percent living in rural
            areas. Approximately one-third of Sweden's pop-
            ulation lives in or near one of Sweden's three
            largest cities, Stockholm, Göteborg, and Malmö.

Capital: Stockholm (metropolitan area population of
            approximately 1.7 million people), located by
            the lake Mälaren on the coast of the Baltic Sea
            in the middle-eastern part of Sweden.

Climate: Variations between north and south. Cold in
            the northern parts of the country, and tem-
            perate in the southern and middle parts.

Terrain:	Pine forests in the north, oaks and other leafy trees in the south, lakes and large archipelagos. Mostly flat with hills and blunt mountains in the north. Highest mountain is Kebnekaise at 2117 meters (6946 feet).
Wildlife:	Deer and elk are common. Bear and wolf are found in the north, and occasionally around the Stockholm area.
Resources:	Iron and steel, paper products, hydroelectric power, electronics.
Flag:	A yellow cross on a dark blue background. The Swedish flag dates back to the sixteenth century and was for a long time the king's token of sovereignty. The cross has its origins in the banners carried in the crusades of the medieval Christian princes.
Language:	Swedish. Sweden is considered monolingual, but Finnish and the languages of the Laps are officially recognized minority languages.
Currency:	Krona (crown) and öre. There are 100 öre per krona. For the current exchange rate, visit www.xe.com/ucc/.
Politics:	Constitutional monarchy, led by a prime minister and the Riksdag (Parliament); mainly social democrats.
Religion:	Mainly Evangelical Lutheran (official state religion). Most people do not attend church regularly.

Chapter One

Bronze Age: 1500–500 BC

FROM ICE AGE TO BRONZE AGE

Sweden's history spans fourteen thousand years and starts when the ice cap that covered the region slowly retreated. The climate became warmer, allowing plants and animals to flourish. The first human dwelling dates from around 10,000 BC. Around 7700 BC the southern tip of Sweden was habitable to humans, and settlers arrived in larger numbers from the Danish islands in the south via the land bridge to Scandinavia. Based on artifacts found in the north, it is also speculated that people migrated south from the northeastern parts of the region, and from Russia. The first human inhabitants were hunters and gatherers. Between 8000 and 6000 BC, as the ice retreated further from the coasts, more settlers arrived inland from the south as well as from the east. This time period, up to approximately 1800 BC, is referred to as the Stone Age.

The first humans lived in caves, used simple tools of stone for hunting and fishing, and later built huts and smaller communities. But they were still nomadic and moved from place to place in their hunt for food, mostly fish, fruits, nuts, bird eggs, and on occasion meat of seal or deer. During this era, men and women functioned mostly as equals, as the group they provided for was small and the children few in a world where starvation and death were always near.

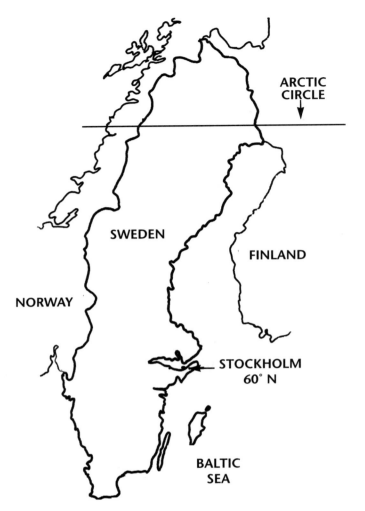

ARCTIC
CIRCLE

SWEDEN

FINLAND

NORWAY

STOCKHOLM
60° N

BALTIC
SEA

Because of Sweden's latitudinal extent, the country has a couple of climate regions. The northern part is marked by harsh winters, while the southern part has a milder climate. Sweden's capital, Stockholm, is located at approximately the same latitude as Anchorage, Alaska, but the warm Gulf Stream in the Atlantic gives Stockholm a warmer climate, with small temperature differences between summer and winter. In today's Sweden, the average winter temperature in Stockholm is 29 degrees F, and the average summer temperature is 63 degrees F. For comparison, the average yearly temperature in Anchorage is 36 degrees F. Note that the Arctic Circle cuts through the northern part of Sweden.

In their struggle for survival, the people invented more sophisticated tools and made clothes out of animal skins and furs. Around 3000 BC the people domesticated deer, hogs, goats, and cows, and life become a bit more secure. But dropping temperatures required southward migration to more favorable climates at the coasts and Baltic islands. As a result, contacts between southern Scandinavia and the European continent became more frequent. Movement with the seasons still characterizes Swedish culture, today more out of preference than necessity.

The time period that followed is called the Bronze Age, 1500–500 BC, which is really the beginning of civilized society in Sweden, and where this book begins.

THE BEGINNING OF SOCIETY

Sweden lagged behind the rest of Europe in development for a considerable part of its history. At the start of the Swedish Bronze Age, the more sophisticated societies around the Mediterranean were already moving into the Iron Age. The Bronze Age in Sweden is symbolized by the use of weapons, primarily axes, spears, and swords made of bronze. Prehistoric sites contribute much of what we know about the late Stone Age and Bronze Age. Such sites are common, especially in the lower third of Sweden along the coast as well as inland, and contain rock carvings, stone burial cairns, and archaeological finds, including tools of stone and bronze, and ornaments and jewelry such as pins and necklaces. In addition to using bronze for tools, archaeologists suggest that bronze was used to indicate a person's rank or status as chief or warrior.

The Bronze Age is also symbolized by the domestication of horses and farm animals, and the use of woolen clothing.

Rock carvings picturing daily life with the sun disk, plowing farmers, animals, and boats are usually found on large sloping rocks facing toward meadows. There is debate as to whether the boats represent real boats, or are merely symbols of commerce or religious concepts.

Farming gave people an annual supply of food. It created stability and therefore a more structured society. But farming required advanced tools. Early rock carvings from southern Sweden depict ships as well as farmers plowing the fields. These images may indicate a culture with trade links and continental communications. Bronze was a vital import, acquired from the more advanced societies in middle and southern Europe, often in exchange for *bärnsten* (amber), a golden fossilized resin of ancient trees that can be found around the Baltic Sea.

THE HOME—THE CENTER OF LIFE

The home was the center of life and the beginning of society as we know it today. Artifacts from homes and graves have helped identify the value system of this era. Villages consisted of a cluster of buildings surrounded by fields and pastures. The houses functioned both as social gathering places and as centers of production. People lived in *långhus* (longhouses), four-sided houses with timber posts and walls made of intertwined twigs and mud. The sizes of the houses varied, which could indicate their social function, and may have been a way for people to find their identity and rank in a small community.

The people were mainly farmers struggling to end their nomadic lifestyle and settle in a more permanent place. They grew a varied crop, including wheat, barley, rye, and also peas and beans. The variation in grain suggests that the people had connections to Asia, as well as south and west to the British Isles. The ownership of farm animals gave increased security and food and, therefore, the ability to afford more children. Whereas the roles of men and women had previously been nearly equal, women now became responsible primarily for the care of children and the preparation of food, while men were responsible primarily for hunting, fishing, and the care of animals. The women learned to make ceramic jars and bowls for the storage of food, as well as wool cloth that allowed them to exchange heavy animal skins and furs for more lightweight clothing. Finds from Bronze Age graves have established that men wore woolen frocks and mantles, and women wore short-sleeved sweaters, skirts, and hoods or hairnets.

Farming allowed the group to grow and live together for longer periods of time, and the group became known as an *ätt* (family). More people were needed for work and the survival of the community, and the children were of great value. As the *ätt* grew, it divided, until several smaller communities, each called a *stam* (tribe), formed. The men made all the important decisions. The ability to rear animals, farm the earth, live together, and hunt for food resulted in wealth, abundance, and a time of peace.

HIGHER POWERS

As life became more organized, people started looking for a higher power and held ceremonies for the gods in hope that the crops would be good. The people traded animal skins and furs in return for bowls of bronze that could be offered to the gods. If famine struck, they needed a greater offering: a person from their own *ätt*. If times were especially bad, they might sacrifice their leader (literally), or elect another leader.

During prehistoric times (and until the Viking Age) the many tribes were not unified but had their own leaders or kings. Smaller chieftaincies as well as stronger kingdoms existed, with Old Uppsala just north of Stockholm becoming a primary political center. The chieftains were both political and religious leaders elected for their luck in harvest, trade, and hunting, and for their ability to bring peace and defend the people against enemy attacks. Since the chieftains were elected by the people, they could also be dethroned and killed or sacrificed if they failed their people.

The selection of leaders, chosen from among the wisest and most experienced men within the community, led to the establishment of an upper class. Men led men, and women led women in their daily chores. People had their specific work duties, with each *ätt* having its own rules. The individuals living within the *ätt* needed the approval of the *ätt* for their activities. In return, the *ätt* was responsible for the well-being and security of its people. This solidarity was confined to the specific *ätt* one was part of and was not extended to those belonging to a different *ätt*.

Every year, a *blotfest* (blood fest) was held, where relatives of the same tribe met, made offerings to the gods, and traded skins and furs for bronze from foreigners. Bronze, an alloy of copper and tin that is stronger than copper alone, was imported from middle Europe and transported in boats along Sweden's coastline. Bronze was originally used for making better tools, including axes, knives, and scrapers for skins. There was also slave trade, with slaves coming from the less advanced people in the northern part of Sweden.

Toward the end of the Bronze Age, bronze became a luxury used in religious ceremonies and to ornament leaders. The leaders were viewed as half-gods, owned slaves, didn't participate in the daily chores, and used religion to increase their own power and wealth. The leaders decided that bronze was too valuable to be used for tools, and forced the people to go back to manufacturing their everyday tools from bone, wood, and stone.

BURIAL OF THE DEAD

More permanent settlements led to a need to bury the dead. During the Stone Age, they were interred in megalithic graves, consisting of large blocks of stone resting on several smaller blocks. Around 3400 BC the megalithic grave was replaced by the *gånggrift* (passage grave), a way to collectively bury as many as 150 bodies, all supplied with food and tools for their passage to the afterlife. Finds from these graves include flint stone axes and arrowheads, needles made of bone, ceramic bowls, and jewelry, such as beads made of amber.

During the late Stone Age, the *hällekistan* (flat rock tomb) was in use. These graves were built of large flat blocks of stone placed vertically into the ground, with one large block placed horizontally on top like a roof. *Hällekistan* most likely held up to seventy bodies.

During the Bronze Age, the dead were buried in piles of rock, or cairns, that were probably built as monuments to the dead. Many of these piles are found in the western part of Sweden, are often round or oval in shape, and contain a burial chamber in the middle, where the leader or other person of power might have been buried. Most of these cairns were placed on higher land, often near the water, and with a view of the surrounding areas.

By approximately 1000 BC the leaders were buried separately in huge piles of rock, while the rest of the population were buried in smaller piles. Many of the graves were placed at the outer regions of the farmed country, perhaps to indicate the boundary between the living and the dead, or the boundary between the farmed and the wild. Southern Sweden contains large areas of grave mounds that are covered with turf. During the early Bronze Age, several thousands of these graves were raised. But such large graves made much of the land unusable for farming. Around 1000 BC the graves

Model of hällekistan *displayed at the Museum of History in Stockholm.*

became smaller, and people also started cremating their dead. This shift may indicate a new way of looking at life, death, and the journey into the afterlife. When a body was cremated, the soul was set free. Rock carvings in graves commonly show a ship carrying the symbol of the sun (a circle), traveling across the sky during the day and under the earth at night. It is possible that, in addition to symbolizing power and trade, the sun and the ship symbolized the circle of life and death

The idea to raise ships of stone is almost exclusively Scandinavian. During the Bronze Age, the area was rich in water, which created a need for ships as a means of transportation.

The ship had important meaning to the people of this era, and during the late Bronze Age and the Iron Age, it was common to bury the dead in a *skeppssättning* (ship setting), consisting of a number of large stones placed in the shape of a ship, with the tallest stones at the bow and stern. The size of these ships varied in length between six and forty-six meters. The common factor of these "ship burials" is that the dead were cremated and the bone fragments placed in urns.

Ale's Stones in Ystad, Skåne, 58 boulders raised in the outline of a ship.

Photo: www.imagebank.sweden.se © Richard Ryan.

Things underwent a radical change around 500 BC when the use of bronze abruptly halted: a new society emerged. Iron was easier to come by and didn't need to be imported, and when the need for bronze ceased, the ship was no longer needed as an important symbol of trade and commerce.

Chapter Two

Iron Age: 500 BC–AD 800

COLDER CLIMATE

The warmer post-glacier period that had lasted from the later Stone Age ended around 500 BC, and the climate in Sweden became colder and moister, with winters rich in snow. The growth of pine trees spread and took over much of the earlier leafy forests. Colder temperatures required warmer clothing and more intense farming for survival, with rye becoming the dominant grain because of its toughness and ability to endure the harsher climate. The people started to wear trousers for warmth and expanded their houses to accommodate the farm animals that had to be brought inside during the colder months.

Archaeological finds of building foundations show long-houses, generally made of mud and stone, and of varied sizes between 5 and 45 meters long and 7 to 10 meters wide, with the roof supported by rows of coarse poles. Many of these houses contained only one source of heat, generally a flat mud hearth placed in the middle of the house. Some of the larger houses were divided into a living area, a storage room, and a room for the animals. Sometimes the houses were built in groups, with a larger 20 to 30 meter long house at a right angle to a smaller 6 to 10 meter long house.

The old tools made of stone were inadequate for farming and for bringing food inside for the animals, and bronze was expensive and difficult to come by. Iron ore was more common than copper and tin. The Iron Age was initiated when the people learned to handle iron to make better tools and weapons. Initially, the iron had to be imported, which was expensive. But soon the people in Sweden learned to mine their own iron and forge it into strong and sharp tools that were cheaper and more durable than bronze or flint.

The people lived closely together in large families. Often grandparents, sisters and brothers-in-law, their children, and slaves shared a single room with the main family. Ceramic jars and coal from the fireplace, along with finds of food remains from the "garbage dump," containing the bones of cows, pigs, sheep, fish, and birds, give us an idea of what people ate. With so many living together, sanitation became an issue. It is believed that the garbage dump was also used as a toilet. Some of these dumps were a couple of meters deep and located some distance from the main dwelling, perhaps in an attempt to avoid nasty odors and the spread of disease.

When farm animals were slaughtered, the meat was smoked or dried to keep it from rotting. Meat and fish were wrapped in large leaves and placed in a pit containing heated rocks from the fireplace. The pit was covered with sod and turf, allowing the food to cook for several hours. During the later Iron Age, the food was prepared in pots and pans made of iron. Bread was baked in the fireplace ashes, in an oven, or simply on a slab of clay. Raspberries, blueberries, apples, and hazelnuts were also part of the diet, along with milk and beer. *Mjöd* (mead), a very Swedish beer made of honey, yeast, and water, was brewed even in the Bronze Age and became particularly popular later during the Viking Age.

THE SIZE OF THE FAMILY

Around AD 200, the people were able to permanently end their nomadic lifestyle and cultivate the earth for a greater supply of food that lasted year round. This shift also forced

Iron Age ceramic jar displayed at the Museum of History in Stockholm.

the division of the *ätt*, which had now grown too large to feed off a single piece of land. Farming was needed for survival but, according to tradition, the young men must move away to other *ätter* to get married, which also meant the loss of ownership of the farm animals they had acquired. To solve the problem, the young men stayed with the *ätt* they were born into, kept ownership of the animals, and bought themselves women to marry from other *ätter*. When the women had to relocate to their new *ätt*, they lost their right to all ownership and became themselves a sort of property.

Normally, monogamy was practiced. However, writing in runes, the first written language developed around AD 200, sometimes tells of well-off men with more than one wife. The size of a family can sometimes be determined through the runes on gravestones, which often name the children who raised the stone for their parents. The average family consisted of one to three children who reached maturity. Sometimes, children born out of wedlock or slaves who had been freed were adopted into the family. The *ätt*, as a whole, was also responsible for the wellbeing and care of the elderly, sick, and handicapped.

Around AD 400, the people found that they could cultivate the earth better if several large families joined together and divided the land into fields for grazing and farming. A new solidarity between the people was born, with boundaries between families becoming less defined.

CLOTHING FOR DRESS AND PROTECTION

During the earlier Iron Age, cow and sheep skins were still used as coats, but around AD 100, wool became more popular and was used for cloaks and larger pieces of clothing. Wool of different colors (white, gray, black, and brown) was woven into artful patterns. Plant coloring was also used to produce blue and different hues of red.

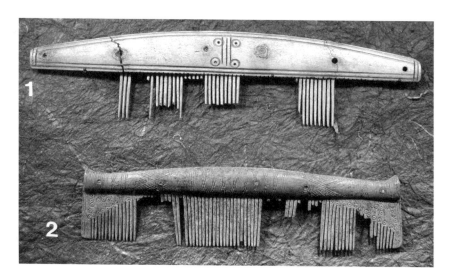

Combs displayed at the Museum at Birka. Combs were usually made of bone or antlers. Some were double-sided, with narrow teeth and less spacing on one side, which may have been used to comb lice from the hair. In today's Sweden, a comb is popularly referred to as lusräfsa *(licerake), perhaps a term that has historical meaning and has survived into the twenty-first century.*

The era's dress, which was practical for the lifestyle and work that needed to be done, consisted of shirts, trousers, tunics, and cloaks of wool. Animal skins and leather were still used, but mainly for protection in warfare. Archaeological finds of combs indicate that people were also concerned both with their looks and their personal hygiene.

Arm rings, neck rings, and buckles were some of the decorative items worn, displayed here at the Museum of History in Stockholm.

DEFENSE AND THE GROWTH OF THE COMMUNITY

All surplus crops and farm animals were given to the leader of the *ätt* for further division. The people's profits were small, and soon they found themselves with too few cattle to produce the manure needed to enrich the soil. With the farming unbalanced as a result, the people faced harder times with not enough food for their families. When the surplus ran out and they were unable to fulfill the increasing requirements of the leader, they were forced to go to war and plunder other *ätter* in distant terrain. The people built forts for protection against plunderers and used fire to warn of the approaching enemy.

The original Eketorps Fortress, with a diameter of fifty-seven meters, was built around AD 300. A hundred years later, the fortress was rebuilt to a diameter of eighty meters, containing around fifty smaller houses. Twenty-six thousand artifacts of common objects for daily use, including jewelry and weapons, have been found within its walls.

In an attempt to protect against plunderers, several families from *ätter* who were not blood related often joined together and broke the leader's power. They could now keep the surplus for themselves. The society that emerged chose a new leader and established the *ting* (a court), an assembly of free men that met regularly and decided on important issues regarding the ownership and division of private and common property of goods and land. The *ting* decided where to draw boundaries between the ownership of farms and fishing waters, resolved conflicts between *ätter*, and helped with the defense of the community. The *ting* legislated and judged in accordance with laws that had been memorized. Although the idea was the equal right to vote for all free men, most likely the richest members of the community influenced the decisions made at the *ting*.

Around AD 500, several communities united in an attempt to reach even greater strength and defensive capabilities. One of the leaders was chosen as king, probably based on his strength and luck with harvest, trade, and defense against enemies. The different leaders and the king received gifts from the people on a voluntary basis. Now that the power was in the hands of the people, they could keep much of their surplus. They had food and time left over after the day's work and could develop better tools. Newer tools, teamwork, and the sharing of land created a village with increased production capabilities. The leaders and the king owned slaves captured during warfare, or children of slaves, to handle the farming. The slaves were considered foreigners, received only room and board for their work, and were exempt from normal laws. Their presence marked the beginning of a class-structured society. Side-by-side with the free farmers emerged a new class of people: those who owned nothing and worked for others. In comparison to the free farmers, the slaves were few in number.

THE GREAT MIGRATIONS

During the time of peace that followed, the people shaped iron into newer and stronger tools, such as axes, knives, scissors, planes, needles, tongs, and sledgehammers. The manufacturing of tools developed alongside farming, especially in areas rich in iron ore. Foreigners from other areas arrived and traded food and furs for iron, which led to communication and teamwork between people living far apart. Sweden entered into greater communications with the Mediterranean societies. Writings by Publius Cornelius Tacitus, a Roman writer, tell

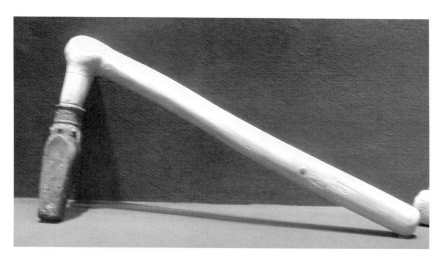

This axe, displayed at the Museum of History in Stockholm, was a luxury item not used by the common man.

about the Svear (Swedes) and the country Svitjod (Sweden), and how the Svear used their fleet, soldiers, and military organization to expand their kingdom toward the other Baltic countries. Large amounts of silver coins from the Roman Empire have been found in Sweden.

Around AD 300, a troublesome period erupted when the Huns, a group of nomadic warlike people from north-central Asia terrorized, plundered, and destroyed much of Europe, forcing migration and conflicts between tribes. With war and plundering came plague epidemics that killed one-third of Europe's population. The great migrations lasted in Europe until around AD 600, and in Sweden mainly between AD 400 and 550.

The period that followed is called *vendeltid*, named after the parish of Vendel Kyrka (a church) along the river Vendel in Uppland in the middle part of Sweden, and is symbolized by relative peace. During this era, elegant weapons and armor were manufactured for the leaders, but were probably used more as symbols of status than for actual warfare. Several archaeological finds from around the church show remains of the mightiest rulers of the time, buried in seven to ten meter long rowboats that had been readied for warfare. The bodies were not cremated but buried with full body armor and helmet, sword, food and drink, and in one, even a board game with pieces made of ivory.

During the Iron Age, the Swedes embraced a polytheistic heathen religion. The Iron Age ended with the start of the Viking Age around AD 800. The introduction of Christianity came soon after, around AD 1000.

Iron Age or early Viking Age helmet displayed at the Museum of History in Stockholm.

Chapter Three

Viking Age: AD 800–1050

IMPORTANT TRADE

The Viking Age is typically seen as the end of the prehistoric era in the Nordic countries and is identified by trading and plundering voyages with origins in Svea Rike, as well as in Denmark, Norway, and Iceland. The Vikings came from all of Scandinavia and went wherever a ship could carry them. The territory that is Sweden today looked much different during the Viking Age; its borders changed constantly throughout its history. The area the Vikings occupied may be understood better in terms of their trading routes than in terms of land. While the Vikings who went westward to Britain and France were mostly Danish and Norwegian, the Swedish Vikings traded mostly with southern and eastern Europe and with Asia. We will try to stick to the history of the Swedish Vikings as much as possible, but keep in mind that many of the events overlap. Swedes, Danes, and Norwegians spoke a common language—Norse—and shared a common culture.

"Free us, O Lord, from the frenzy of the Norsemen." The Vikings were fierce warriors and feared by many, as is expressed in the prayers of the French. We tend to picture the Vikings as war-loving, plundering, greedy, ruthless, dirty beasts wearing helmets with horns, sailing the seas in long ships with a shallow keel, and spreading havoc among the inhabitants of

Sweden during late Viking Age, Middle Ages, and early twentieth century. Territorially, the Swedish Vikings' base was in Uppland and centered around Old Uppsala north of the lake Mälaren.

other nations. However, for the purposes of this study, when talking about Vikings, we mean mainly the people who lived in Sweden around AD 800–1050. Raids and plundering were part of the culture, gave status and economic power, and were not limited to the Nordic countries. In addition, plundering, destruction, and warfare were often followed by construction and achievement.

It is believed trade, raids, and warfare accounted for less than 20 percent of the country's economic undertakings. Most Vikings did not live solely off of their commerce and plundering. Farming was still the main source of livelihood. Shortages at home, and the knowledge that they were superior at sea, may have contributed to the Vikings' plundering voyages. Other theories are that they desired freedom and detested being bound by kings and other rulers.

The Swedes had, in the centuries preceding the Viking Age, established trade with far away countries, mainly to the east and south along the European continent. Around AD 800, the main trading post re-located to Birka, the first Swedish city, on Björkö in Mälaren, the lake in middle Sweden. Birka was located on the main shipping route, with inlets from the Baltic Sea. A prosperous merchant class emerged, and the trading engagements became more regular. The ruins at Birka are tangible evidence of a strong commercial center and show trading with both east and west. With a population of 700–1000, Birka became one of the most significant cities in northern Europe. It remained an important trading post for two hundred years and is today a site of continuous archaeological excavation.

As a result of plundering voyages, colonization in other countries, and access to commerce, Sweden went through a dynamic economic development during the Viking Age. With the advent of the sailing ship, the people were able to communicate and trade on the international level. Sweden, alongside the other Nordic countries, became a leader in commerce between western Europe and the Orient. During the later part of the Viking Age, Swedish cities functioned as centers of economy and politics.

The Swedes focused on acquiring silver in the form of coins, and jewelry from Baghdad and the Arab world in exchange for furs, honey, amber, wax, weapons, and slaves. Finds from Gotland (the larger of the two islands east of the south tip of Sweden) account for more than half of all the silver finds in Sweden, including more than 140,000 silver coins. Most of these coins date to around AD 900 and are of Islamic, German, and English design. Gotland is therefore believed to have been a supply stop for the Vikings, and an important link to seafaring and trade.

In addition to silver coins, jewelry in the form of rings and bracelets has been found in large amounts, stowed away in leather pouches and boxes dug down in fields and under the floorboards of ruined buildings. Why the treasures were hidden, never claimed, and found a thousand years later is up for debate. It could be the effect of widespread disturbances in the region, where endangered people found a need to hide their valuables. The coins were often grouped according to weight, which suggests that the value of silver in weight was more important than the value stated on the coin. It is believed that the large amount of silver was acquired both through commerce and plundering.

The trade routes went from the Baltic along western European rivers to the Mediterranean Sea, and on the bigger rivers of the Volga and the Dnepr to the Caspian and Black seas. When reaching shallower waters, the Vikings pulled their ships up on land and carried or rolled them on tree logs. Many of the ships that have been recovered show a worn keel, an indication that the ships were dragged ashore. The Vikings'

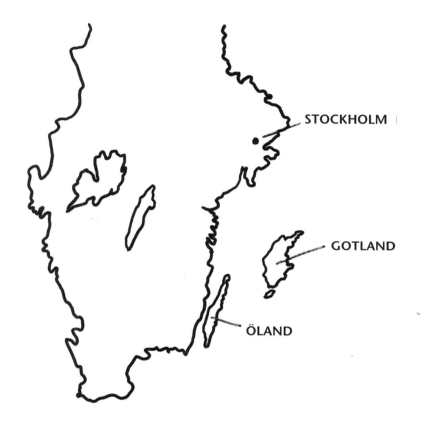

The islands of Öland and Gotland are located at Sweden's south tip. Gotland, the larger of the two, has revealed particularly large finds of silver.

A Viking Age silver find displayed at the Museum at Birka.

extensive communication links included western Europe, the British Isles, India, and Russia. Cities grew along the way, and finds from grave mounds, primarily in Staraja Ladoga, Novgorod, and Smolensk in Russia suggest the establishment of Nordic colonies. Novgorod and Kiev were important stations on the Vikings' way to Persia and Byzantium. Around AD 900, the trade with central and western Europe grew. At the same time the trade with the Arab world ended, apparently because hostile Slavic tribes in southern Russia forced the Vikings to be both traders and warriors, making it hazardous to travel in smaller parties.

The Vikings were most likely relatively peaceful when home between voyages. However, they were also feared and dangerous warriors, unafraid to die in combat. They were known for their loyalty and courage, and were often employed as guards to kings in foreign countries. When they sailed the Black Sea and attacked Constantinople, the Byzantine emperors were impressed with the Vikings' ferocity and recruited them for the Varangian Guard, an elite guard for the emperor.

THE SHIP, THE BAY, AND THE RAID

The exact meaning of the word Viking has been debated many times. Some suggest that it stems from *vik*, the Swedish word for bay. Viking may therefore mean "bayer," or one who is capable of sailing a ship into the shallow waters of the bay. An important feature of the Viking ship was its lack of a significant keel. An alternative interpretation is "merchant" in accordance with the Latin word *vicus* (village), or one who traveled to other cities and villages to trade and acquire goods. The people east of the Baltic (which is now Russia) used the word *Rus* to describe the Vikings. The Rus gave their name to Russia and founded the first Russian state centered on Kiev, which also became the stronghold of the Rus. *Ruotsi,* the Finnish term for Swedes, meaning rowing way, or oarsmen, may also be related. Another common word is *Väringar*, which refers to the people who served in the Byzantine Empire as guards to the emperor. However, the most common image the word Viking evokes is probably that of a sea pirate or warrior. The word Viking might therefore have been a verb rather than a noun. To go "i-Viking" meant to embark on an expedition of piracy and plunder.

Much of the fame of the Vikings may lie in the superiority of their ships. They were designed primarily for maneuverability and speedy transport of warriors with the help of the wind, and built so that they could travel in both shallow and deep waters. The Viking ships were long and slender, commonly twenty-three meters long and five meters wide, and built of wood, either oak or pine, with overlapping planking joined together by iron nails. The thin planking made the hull flexible, to work with the forces of the sea. We know as much as we do about the look and design of the Viking ships because well-off men were often buried with their ships when they died. To date, the longest ship found is thirty-six meters. The Nordic people started using sails around AD 500, and by the time the Viking Age rolled around, it is estimated that the ships were capable of traveling at speeds of 12–14 knots, with an average speed of 6–8 knots. Square sails made of wool or linen, with tar and fat added to produce stiffness and water resistance, made it possible for the Vikings to expand their voyages. The ships were also suited to operate with rowers, between twelve and twenty pairs working in unison, depending on the size and primary voyage of the ship.

The ships were capable of crossing the Atlantic, as well as traveling along the rivers in Europe. Harbors were unnecessary, as they could sail all the way into the bay and easily be pulled up on the beach and rolled on tree logs a short distance across the terrain. The Vikings also used anchors made of iron. Wider and roomier ships were used as freighters, designed for commerce rather than speed.

The Vikings' ability to enter shallow waters was instrumental to their success. The Vikings often used surprise tactics and quick plundering raids, winning many battles because of their swiftness and superiority at sea. When horses were brought along, locations further inland could be reached quickly, and before the population had time to mount a defense, the Vikings had already plundered the villages and

Viking ship pictured on rune stone displayed at the Museum of History in Stockholm.

Model of Viking ship displayed at the Museum at Birka.

set back out to sea. The raids consisted both of smaller parties and of larger fleets of ships. During the plundering raids, the Vikings acquired slaves to trade for silk, jewelry, and spices in southern Europe, or to be sold as labor to the silver mines in the Middle East.

The Vikings manufactured spears, axes, and swords of iron, often decorated with copper or silver. For defense in man-to-man combat, they used a round shield made of wood covered with leather, and with an iron plate in the center to protect the hand. In most archaeological finds, only the centerpiece of iron remains. Contrary to popular belief, the Vikings did not wear helmets with horns in combat. The helmet was generally made of iron with a shielding faceguard. A leather hood was sometimes worn underneath the helmet. The shield was the primary defense, with helmets or chain mail used mostly by the wealthier Vikings.

While the men were away on their voyages, the women and sometimes the slaves stayed behind and tended to the farm. At times, regular farmers also worked as rowers on the ships. Courage was valued, and the warriors followed those leaders they believed to be blessed with good luck. During longer voyages to foreign countries, the different kings and leaders combined their warriors into a bigger army, forming fleets of several ships to further strengthen their power. Some of the Vikings became so rich that they could move away from their king and former village to build a separate home for their wife, children, and slaves.

The Vikings traveled both to the west and east, up the large rivers of the Rhine, Seine, Rhone, and Loire. They sailed into the English Channel, and in AD 793 raided the Lindisfarne monastery on Holy Island on England's northeastern coast. Monks were killed, altars sabotaged, and valuable objects stolen. This attack was the first against English territory that can be verified through written documents and was recorded in the Anglo-Saxon Chronicle: "The harrying heathen destroyed God's church in Lindisfarne by rapine and slaughter." Some see the attack on Holy Island as the defining factor of the start of the Viking Age.

The trick in defending against the Vikings lay in the ability to detect and interfere with the raids at sea, prior to the ships reaching the beach. When the western European countries had built a significant system of defense, consisting of a coast guard and fleet, they could be forewarned of the attacks and meet the Viking raids at sea. When the Vikings could no longer find unprotected coasts and defenseless towns, they lost much of their power. When professional armies became the rule rather than the exception throughout western Europe, the foundation for the Vikings' success was uprooted and that may be the primary reason the raids ended around AD 1050. Increased business practice within the Nordic countries may have been a second reason the Viking Age was brought to an end.

EVERYDAY LIFE

Many Vikings were accomplished in both trade and warfare, and many were primarily traders. When out on their voyages, they might also have been tempted to pirate smaller ships that happened to come their way, and they carried weapons and armor for this purpose, as well as for defense. However, most Vikings were regular folks abiding by the rules of society and living in accordance with a democratic system of decision-making.

The Vikings had families, lived in villages or in single houses set distances apart in southern and middle Sweden, and farmed and raised cattle between voyages.

Homes were built primarily of wood with a separate room or different house for the animals. Model displayed at the Museum at Birka.

The Vikings were concerned about the welfare and honor of their families. In the winter months, they manufactured new tools, mended fishing nets, and made clothing of wool. When spring came, they worked the fields and let the cattle out to feed. The standard of living increased dramatically during the Viking Age. Better climate and more modern farm tools contributed to a heavy increase in the population, with new villages growing up near the old. Despite the focus on the family, it is believed that both plural marriage and divorce were allowed.

Society consisted of an upper class of rich and free farmers who owned ships and large areas of land, a middle class of regular farmers who owned smaller pieces of land and cattle, and slaves who owned nothing and worked long hours for others in return for room and board. The slaves were divided into three classes: those who were too poor to provide for themselves, prisoners of war, and children born into slavery. Sometimes slaves could buy their freedom after many years of hard work. Later, when the hunt for slaves had ended both in and out of the country, existing slaves became a valuable commodity. As a result, they dared to challenge their owners and refuse to work as they had in the past. Since many slave owners resented the idea of doing their own farming, they were forced into an agreement with the slaves. Many slaves now became half-owned and half-free, and could gain their full freedom with time. The slaves acquired the right to build a family and move to a cottage where they could farm a piece of land for own use.

Most of the information regarding the status of women stems from rune stones and archaeological finds. It is believed that during the Viking Age Nordic women were valued and honored, did not suffer from oppression by men, and had in general more freedom and power than the women of other

European countries. It is believed that the women were in charge of the finances and made the decisions about the work and household duties. For example, merchant's scales have been found in female graves, indicating that women frequently partook in commerce and trading within the community.

The men were responsible for bringing food to the table and were skilled fishermen and hunters of deer, bear, and wild hogs. But when the men were away on their voyages, the women had to take on greater responsibilities at home and do the men's work as well as their own, cooking, childcare, spinning, and weaving. Increased responsibilities led to increased power, even in downtime between voyages. One theory is that a woman's status increased with age, while a man's status decreased with age. The man's role was grounded in physical strength and ability to participate in warfare, while the woman's role was grounded in wisdom and experience. If a man died, his wife and children inherited the farm, and the wife was responsible for the children until they were old enough to set out on their own.

Most people wore plain clothing with few details. The rich and the poor could be distinguished through the material of their clothing rather than by the style or details of dress. Regular folks wore wool, and the upper classes wore silk or velvet. The clothing was mostly homemade, and shoes were simple and made out of leather. Both men and women enjoyed beautiful jewelry and ornaments. Rather than using buttons to hold clothes together, they used buckles, pins, and brooches, and wore jewelry in the form of necklaces, bracelets, and rings, sometimes decorated with amber.

Although Ibn Fadlan, an Arab chronicler, has described the Vikings as: "The filthiest of God's creatures. They have no modesty in defecation and urination, nor do they wash after pollution from orgasm, nor do they wash their hands after

Merchant's scale displayed at the Museum at Birka.

Elaborate Viking Age brooch. The pin or brooch that held the garments together may have been the most important decorative item.

Viking Age jewelry displayed at the Museum of History in Stockholm.

eating," personal hygiene and grooming is believed to have been relatively good, including hand washing before and after meals.

Ibn Fadlan goes on to say: "I have seen the Rus as they came on their merchant journeys and encamped by the Volga. I have never seen more perfect physical specimen, tall as date palms, blonde and ruddy; they wear neither tunics nor caftans, but the men wear a garment, which covers one side of the body and leaves a hand free. The Rus are a great host, all of them red haired; they are big men with white bodies." The garment, which "covers one side of the body and leaves a hand free," was most likely the Norse rectangular cloak, which was pinned at the right shoulder, leaving the sword-hand free.

The Vikings ate two meals a day, one in the morning to give them strength to carry out the day's chores, and one in the evening. The family and invited guests, such as traveling merchants, often gathered around and ate directly from a big pot containing the

Viking Age warrior wearing the era's rectangular cloak, which was pinned at the right shoulder, leaving the sword-hand free. Displayed at the Museum at Birka.

47

food. The pot hung from the ceiling over a burning fire that also kept the house warm. Boiled meat or fish flavored with salt and garlic were common in addition to porridge and vegetables such as cabbage and peas. Food was also stored to last through the winter, and smoked or preserved with ice or salt obtained from boiling salt water. Although the Vikings are often portrayed as brutal warriors, writings on rune stones have revealed the Vikings' hospitality toward non-hostile strangers, who often found room and board with families.

The children did not attend school but worked at home and helped on the farm. The Vikings enjoyed physical activities, such as ball games, knife throwing competitions, rock climbing, and wrestling. Upper class children learned swimming, riding, fencing, and archery. Activities that stimulated the mind were also popular, including board games with pieces of ceramic or bone.

WRITTEN COMMUNICATION

The Vikings spoke Norse, a Germanic language, and were called Norsemen. Few detailed Norse writings have been found, most engraved on stones. Around 3500 rune stones and rock carvings have been found in Sweden. Stones were raised as monuments to the dead and often told brief stories of where the Vikings had been or how they lived, but more often the message was simple. A stone found in Sigtuna just north of Stockholm reads: *Ofeg let raise this stone after his two sisters, Tora and Rodvi.*

The original rune alphabet, called the older *futharken* after the first six characters, was developed from a southern European alphabet around AD 200, contained twenty-four characters, and was in use until around AD 800. During the Viking

Age, the alphabet was simplified to sixteen characters and called the younger *futharken*.

The runes were written mainly with straight lines. Since they were originally carved into wood, straight lines were preferred over rounded ones, which were more difficult to carve against the grain. Wood had its advantages over paper or parchment, as the medium was readily available; however, carving made longer writings cumbersome.

Later, when rock carving became more common, the runic alphabet was adapted and new signs developed to complete the alphabet. Carving into stone allowed for more rounded characters. Runes were also carved into bone and metal.

ᚠᚢ ᚦᚨᚱᚲ ᚺᚾᛁᛏ ᛋ ᛏᛒᛘᛚᛦ

f u th a r k   h n i a   s   t b m l   r

The younger futharken. *Note how the lines are at right or diagonal angles. Note also that there are two symbols for the letter* a. *Many of the symbols have more than one sound. For example,* k *can sound like "k" and "g." The first* a *can sound like "o" and "å", and the second* a *can also be "ä." The modern Swedish alphabet is the same as the English alphabet, but has three additional letters (å, ä, ö) tagged on at the end. The letter* å *is pronounced similarly to "oa" in* soar, ä *is pronounced similarly to "ai" in* hair, *and* ö *is pronounced similarly to "i" in* sir *or "e" in* her.

RELIGION AND MYTHOLOGY

Prior to the introduction of Christianity, the Vikings embraced asatro, a polytheistic religion. They believed in several gods; Tor, the god of thunder, and Oden, the god of war, were probably the most familiar ones. Tor was the kind of god who was easily angered, which he expressed through thunder and lightning. The farmers worshipped Tor, who fought evil giants and threw his hammer against them to keep them from taking over the world. The leaders and warriors worshipped Oden, the god of war. Oden sacrificed one of his eyes in exchange for the privilege to drink from the well of Mimer, giving him the wisdom to see into the future.

While the ordinary farmers worshipped the gods of peace and fertility, and believed that wellness came from teamwork within the village rather than from force and war, the Vikings believed that dying in battle was the ultimate aim, and that such a death would reward them with a glorious afterlife. The Valkyries (warrior-maidens) carried the war heroes who died in battle to Valhall in Asgård (the gods' dwelling), where they were allowed to eat and drink and feast for eternity. Those who died at home instead of in battle went to Hel (hell, or the giants' dwelling). Dying in war gave you a better shot at a pleasant afterlife, and the belief in Valhall was a motivating factor for the courageous warriors of this time.

EARLY CHRISTIANITY

The first Christian missionary who visited Sweden is said to have been St. Ansgar, a Saxon monk born in AD 801. St. Ansgar went to Sweden in AD 829, engaged in missionary work at Birka, and built the first Christian church. But the Swedes

Neck ornament with three of Tor's mighty Mjölner (hammer). The hammer was often worn as a pendant by his followers. Displayed at Museum at Birka.

Viking Age glass. The glass was found at a burial site and has escaped damage. Displayed at the Museum at Birka.

The Ansgar Chapel at Birka.

were reluctant to give up their pagan beliefs, and the first missionaries who came to Sweden were soon forgotten. Ansgar's successor, Gautberg, had to leave Birka in AD 839 when riots broke out, his house was demolished, and his nephew was killed by anti-Christians. The missionary work resulted in a struggle between Christianity and paganism. To the Vikings, Tor's hammer was more important than the cross of Christ, and violence between pagans and Christians was common and continued until around AD 1100.

The missionaries from middle Europe tried for two hundred years to convert the Swedes to Christianity. This new religion didn't appeal to common people. The general feeling among them was that in the Christian religion, God was all-powerful, and the people worked for and were obligated to Him much in the same sense that slaves were obligated to their owners. Christianity didn't gain much of a foothold, until the king got baptized and gave land to the bishops, who built churches of wood with steeples of stone. The Christian Church survived, just like the *stormän* (an upper class nobility) did, on ownership of land and labor.

Since early in the Iron Age, the province of Uppland had played an important role as the center of Svea Rike. Later, between AD 1150 and AD 1300, the stone churches that characterize Uppland were built. Around AD 980, King Erik Segersäll founded the city of Sigtuna. Sigtuna has kept much of its original character into modern day. The streets and division of the blocks are much the same as when the city was founded. Several church ruins and rune stones suggest that Sigtuna is where Christianity made its breakthrough, and that the city served as a religious and political center. Sigtuna was Sweden's most prominent city until outclassed by Stockholm, the current capital, around AD 1300.

The remnants of St. Olof's Church in Sigtuna just north of Stockholm. The church was built around AD 1100.

St. Olof's Church is one of the oldest church ruins in Sweden. The church was built in early AD 1100, but could be even older. During archaeological excavation in the summer of 2001, stone walls and a second floor were discovered below the current floor, suggesting that an earlier version of the church exists underneath the ruin. Three graves were also discovered, the oldest of which holds the skeleton of a female dating to late AD 900.

BRIEF MONEY HISTORY

Swedish money has existed for about a thousand years. Prior to minting their own, the Swedes used foreign coins, often Arabic, counting the weight in silver rather than the value stated on the coin. The first Swedish coin was minted in Sigtuna in AD 995 by Olof Skötkonung (son to Erik Segersäll), after English design. At first, the money was minted at several locations. Since roads were nearly non-existent, a central mint would have made it difficult to transport the money to the different provinces. Upon Olof Skötkonung's death in AD 1022, and until about AD 1140, no new money was minted.

For the next five hundred years, only small silver coins, with the largest weighing about one gram, were minted in Sweden. It wasn't until later, under the reign of King Gustav Vasa, 1521–1560, that increased commerce in Europe demanded larger coins. During those years, copper was added to the silver, which devalued the coin and led to inflation.

The value of money was counted according to the Vikings' system of weight. One mark, weighing approximately 210 grams, was divided into 192 *penningar* (derived from the Latin *pecus* meaning cattle, which was the original "money" used in trade for goods or services), 8 *öre*, or 24 *örtugar* (one *örtug* was equal to one-third ounce of silver). There were 8 *penningar* per *örtug*, or 24 *penningar* per *öre*. The provinces

Drawing of Viking Age coin at the Museum of History in Stockholm.

differed somewhat in their ways of counting money, but around 1200 the system was unified and lasted until 1776.

In 1534, Sweden started minting *daler* (note the similarity in the name to *dollar*), renamed *riksdaler* in 1776 and minted until 1873. The first Swedish bills were printed in 1661. Sweden founded the world's first central bank, the *Riksbank*, in 1668, and Sweden was the first European country to use paper money (notes) instead of coins. The primary purpose of printing notes was to avoid heavy transports and storage of coins. By 1832, Sweden finally acquired a central mint, and all minting and printing of money took place in Stockholm. Not until 1873, when Sweden, Denmark, and Norway formed a monetary union, did the current money of *krona* (crown) and *öre* come into existence. The monetary union was dissolved in 1914 with the start of World War I, but all three countries kept crowns as their currency.

As of the writing of this book, Sweden has not yet joined the European Monetary Union and maintains its own currency of *kronor* (crowns) and *öre*. There are 100 *öre* per crown. The smallest coin currently in use in Sweden is 50 *öre*. In the late 1960s and early '70s, when the author was a child, *ettöringar* (coins with the value of one *öre*) existed. You could buy a piece of gum or caramel for five *öre*, and a good size bag of candy for one crown.

THE LAW

Toward the end of the Viking Age, many of the Vikings adjusted to a more structured society and became *stormän*, a social class that lived off of the work of the slaves. The kings still owned most of the land, but the more successful Vikings formed *stormannaklassen* (big man's class). *Stormän* from different provinces had more in common with each other than

From left to right: one öre (no longer in use), 50 öre (front and back, note the three crowns on the back), one crown, and a modern one-hundred-crown bill, picturing Carl von Linne, (Carolus Linnaeus, 1707–78), a Swedish botanist and physician, considered by some the "Father of Botany."

with their poorer relatives, with the upper class children marrying the children of other nobles.

The Swedish provinces grew around villages where the people felt belonging and camaraderie, spoke the same dialect, and had the same traditional values. The law differed between provinces and was enforced by the people who lived under it. Regular meetings at the *ting* (court) were held; chieftains were elected; and laws were declared, memorized, and recited aloud by the law speaker. All free men and women were allowed to speak at the *ting*. Women were generally held to be the equal of men under the law. For example, married women had the right to manage their own money and could also divorce their husbands under the same laws that applied to men. Women also had a right to an inheritance if no male heir existed. Writings on rune stones attest that when a *storman* who lacked male children died, the property went to his sisters or other females in the family. This was done in order to keep the ownership of land within wealthy families.

Honor, truth, and duty were valued, and the penalty for wrongdoing was based on already established laws. The punishment was generally executable by the victim. For example, if somebody was killed, the victim's family was responsible for avenging the death by killing the murderer. Defamation or insult was one of the worst offenses, where the victim had the right to challenge the offender to a duel with the sword. Some insults were considered so grave that they gave the victim the right to take the life of the offender. Theft was another serious crime, punished by hanging. Offenses of a lesser degree could result in the criminal getting his head shaved and his body rolled in tar. If a person committed a crime and was sentenced, he was expected to accept the penalty with courage.

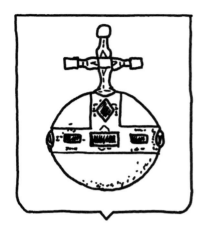

The coat-of-arms of Uppland, where Sweden's rulers have always resided, depicts an orb bearing a cross, symbolizing that the monarch is granted his office by God.

In 1296, a twelve-man committee developed *Upplandslagen* (the law of Uppland). The committee incorporated the already valid laws and founded new laws according to need. *Upplandslagen* served as a forerunner to the modern legal system and had great importance to the implementation of future laws for the provinces.

A seal symbolized each province. A coat-of-arms was later added at the death of King Gustav Vasa in 1560. *Riksregalierna* (the regalia), symbols of the Swedish kingdom and of the monarch as head of state, are comprised of the sword, the crown, the scepter, the orb, and the key. The sword, which was purchased by Gustav Vasa, is the oldest of the regalia. The others date from the coronation of his eldest son in 1561. The sword symbolizes the king's duty to protect good and punish evil. The crown is an emblem of regal honor. The scepter symbolizes the secular power of the king. The orb shows that God granted the king his office. And, finally, the key symbolizes the king's power to harbor good and exclude evil.

OLOF SKÖTKONUNG

The opposition against the Vikings, both at home and in other countries, eventually ended their plundering of wealth and acquisition of slaves. The Vikings stayed home more, and their presence led to a new union between the villages and a more permanent establishment of different *landskap* (provinces, later to unite and become Sweden). Many Vikings were leaders or kings and had interests in their particular *landskap*. Other Vikings were mainly interested in increasing their own private wealth and chose to continue their raids, plundering in the Nordic waters.

Bloody battles followed. One erupted on the field Fyrisvallarna in the province of Uppland in AD 983, when an army of farmers under the leadership of Erik Segersäll (Erik the Victorious) claimed victory over a large army of Vikings. Erik Segersäll also gained victory over the Danish king and acquired Skåne (which is now southern Sweden) and Denmark. He was baptized there but later reverted back to the heathen religions.

Sweden lost Skåne and Denmark again when Erik Segersäll died in AD 995. The monarchy was handed down to his son, Olof Eriksson "Skötkonung," the first officially recognized king of both the Svear (around the lake Mälaren) and the Götar (to the south). Still, Sweden was not yet an integrated state, and the Svear and Götar had difficulties agreeing on a joint king.

Note the name: Olof Eriksson was Erik's son. Many Swedes have last names ending with "son." If you were a man, your last name would be your father's first name with the addition of "son"; for example, the sons of Sven, Ingvar, and Sture would have last names of Svensson, Ingvarsson, and Sturesson. Spelling varies with individual taste. Sometimes one *s* is used and other times two. There is some debate about the meaning

In 1658, Sweden had twenty-four landskap *(provinces), but later added one more for a total of twenty-five. Uppland is located right around Stockholm, Sweden's capital. Except for their traditional value, the provinces play little role in modern Swedish society.*

of the name, Skötkonung, but the most reasonable explanation is that it stems from *skattekonung*, meaning "treasure king," since he was the first king to mint money in Sweden.

It is said that Olof Skötkonung was baptized in AD 1008 by the British missionary bishop Sigfrid (the exact year and the name of the missionary are uncertain). Skötkonung is generally given credit for being the king who Christianized Sweden. When he became Christian, he was banned from pagan Svealand and forced to seek refuge in Skara in Götaland. Sweden's first bishopric was established there later.

When Sweden adopted Christianity, the Vikings lost much of their treasured individual freedom. Not the *ting*, where all free men and women had the right to speak, but the nobility now elected the king, and the king had power only with the consent of the upper class. Not until 1319 were the ordinary folks again allowed to participate in the election of the king.

Chapter Four
Early Middle Age: 1050–1300

CHRISTIANITY AND THE STRUGGLE
FOR A CENTRALIZED POWER

The Swedish Middle Age started at the end of the Viking Age, when the *ting* (court) chose Christianity as the new religion. early Middle Age was characterized by struggles for control and the growth of centralized power, located primarily around Mälaren, the lake in Uppland. Compared to the Viking Age, the Swedish Middle Age was a time of depression with constant struggles between the farmers and the upper classes. Instead of the Vikings ruling their own lives and acting on others, the influence of the church acted upon the Swedes.

The church established a bishopric in Gamla Uppsala north of Stockholm in 1164. The organization of the church and the universal character of its belief promoted the unification of the provinces. However, the provinces still had their own laws and administrative powers at the *ting*. The *stormän* (nobility) continued their struggle for the throne, with two main families, the Sverkers and the Eriks, engaged in a conflict that lasted for nearly sixty years. In the meantime, the different provinces attempted to unite. Still, Sweden was not united as a country in the sense it is today.

During the Viking Age, the only social classes that existed were free or slave. With the coming of Christianity, that was

Altar and baptismal font dating to 1160–1190. Displayed at the Museum of History in Stockholm.

Baptismal font dating to around 1200. Displayed at the Museum of History in Stockholm.

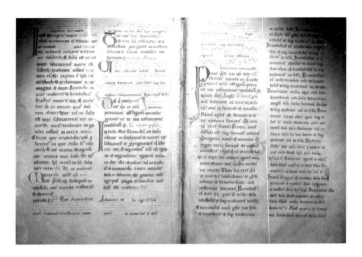

Missal dating to 1198, displayed at the Museum of History in Stockholm.

about to change. The earlier *ätter* (families) were dissolved, and the new society grew into a large number of free farmers and slaves, and a lesser number of *stormän*. Slavery was part of the culture, until 1335 when it was abolished by law , mainly because of the building of cities and the influence of Christianity. When cities were built and a well-defined merchant class emerged, the equality that all free farmers had experienced ended. The farmers could no longer hold the dominant position and lost much of their status.

Christianity made little progress for the first hundred years after its introduction to the Scandinavian countries. The Swedish kings lacked the authority of the leaders of

Sacrament dating to 1200–1400, displayed at the Museum of History in Stockholm.

other European nations and had little success in unifying the country. The local chieftains held the power at the *ting* and had difficulties agreeing on and embracing the new religion. *Stormannaklassen* (big man's class) may have been the first to accept Christianity on social grounds, but it wasn't until the late eleventh century that Christianity began to take hold.

Since the king lacked a centralized palace or residence, communications throughout the country were difficult, and the king was forced to travel around to his different estates. The king's primary residence eventually ended up in Stockholm, where it still is today.

The modern Royal Palace has 550 rooms, but only one balcony!

The king and family live at Drottningholms Slott at the outskirts of the city. The widowed queen Hedvig Eleonora ordered it built in 1662.

LEDUNGEN—
THE FIRST SWEDISH MILITARY

What we know of the early Swedish military stems mostly from rock carvings and archaeological finds, but it is believed that Sweden had mandatory military service already during the Viking Age. All free men had not only the right to bear arms, but also an obligation to partake in the defense of their country or province.

When the Swedish state was formed, the king implemented taxes in support of national defense and crusades. The kingdom, in teamwork with *stormannaklassen*, established a defensive fleet against attacks from the Baltic. This fleet, called *ledungen*, was built on previous knowledge accumulated from the success of the Viking raids and trading voyages. In case of enemy threats, the king would mobilize *ledungen* and guard Sweden's coastline. The provinces were required to supply the king with ships and soldiers. The farmers who lived along the coasts were also required to serve in the fleet, resulting in additional hardship to the farmers who were forced to spend time away from home. The king and *stormän* took the leadership of the fleet and often embarked on crusades to Finland in the east, in an attempt to conquer Finnish land for the Catholic Church. When the king did not call for a crusade, he required the people to pay a tax in place of going to war.

Around 1200, *ledungen* came in need of replacement, partly because the king needed forces within the country to fight against rebellious farmers. The duty to do military service was replaced with a tax, and the money was used for building forts and hiring legionary soldiers.

No legal distinction had been made previously between free men, when in 1280 King Magnus Ladulås issued *Alsnö*

Chess pieces from around 1200, displayed at the Museum of History in Stockholm.

Stadga, a statute that exempted those who could supply the king with an armored soldier and horse from taxation. This elite included the *stormän* as well as the Archbishop and the bishops' men. Through this statute, the king created an army and an upper class, and turned Sweden into a status society with sharp differences between its people. The free farmers paid taxes to the state in addition to the 10 percent they were already paying to the church. The tax-paying farmers had to bear the extra burden of the *frälse* (those who were tax-exempt), and many farmers had to pawn or sell their land to the nobility. The church's tax-exemption had much the same effect. The wealth of priests and church leaders increased, and the upper class became richer and able to buy even more tax-exempt land. As a result, the number of tax-paying people decreased, eventually making it difficult for the state to collect all the money it needed.

ST. ERIK

Whereas the farmers had previously been able to get by on their small pieces of land, the needs of the priests, bishops, and king were ever increasing. Many farmers were forced to borrow from *stormannaklassen*. The transition to Christianity also required that the farmers in each province build a church, choose a priest, and give the bishop and the king some of their grain and farm animals. The costs involved in building churches, paying and maintaining priests, and paying fees for visits from the bishop became a big financial burden that brought the farmers to the brink of starvation. The farmers felt that the Catholic Church and *stormän* robbed them of all they owned. In the meantime, the king and *stormän* supplied the church with gifts and farms, believing the donations would ensure them a place in the afterlife.

When a farmer failed to repay his debts, or was unable to pay the fee to the priest and bishop, he was forced to go to work for a *storman* and give him the farm as collateral. While the farmers were allowed to live on the farm and till the earth, they lost their freedom in the sense that they became employees of the *storman*. Many were also unable to fulfill their duties to the king and, therefore, lost everything they owned, including their right to speak at the *ting*.

In addition to the demands made by the king and *stormän*, the Catholic Church also required that the Swedish people pay Peter's Pence to the pope in Rome. The farmers refused to pay, seeing no profit in sending money to a distant authority. They rebelled and chose a new king, a *storman* by the name of Erik Jedvardsson. In a society where people respected principle more than law, a king who opposed the people's sense of "right" could be dethroned and replaced by another.

When a new king was chosen, he went on Eriksgata, a tour of recognition to receive the allegiance of the people. King

Bromma Kyrka, built during the later half of the twelfth century, is one of the oldest buildings in Stockholm.

Erik was unusual in the sense that he refused to burden the people with taxes. He fought for the Swedish Church's liberation from Rome and for the farmers' right to control their church contributions. But in an ensuing conflict, the Danish prince Magnus Henriksson assassinated King Erik. In 1170, ten years after his death, he became canonized as St. Erik, Sweden's patron saint, but he never received official sainthood from the Catholic Church.

Statue of St. Erik, Sweden's patron saint, displayed at Stockholm City Museum.

The flag of the Swedish Church pictures a red cross on a yellow background, with St. Erik's crown in the middle.

Magnus Henriksson succeeded King Erik and again required of the farmers that they give 10 percent of all grain and newborn animals to the church each year. This tithe drove the farmers into poverty, forcing them to sell their farms and land and work for others. Around 1250, society was so split that it could no longer be ruled by peaceful means. The *stormän* forced the farmers to pay taxes to the king, the king used the money to equip soliders, and the soldiers kept the farmers under control and forbid them to carry weapons. In this sense, the farmers lost their rights as residents and citizens of Sweden. Without the support of the farmers, the *ting* lost much of its power, and the king now made all important decisions.

WRITTEN LAW

The Vikings had lived according to individualistic philosophies and much without constraint, under laws whose purpose was to settle disputes without having to resort to violence. The lawman was responsible for memorizing the laws and reciting them at the *ting*, and for seeking justice. Prior to the Swedish Middle Age, laws existed only orally and differed between provinces. However, although the provinces embraced different laws, they stemmed from common traditions and beliefs.

Written laws were established following several fights between the king and bishops, and between the rulers and the free farmers. The laws were written down in accordance with the wishes of the *stormän*. The accused was guilty until he had proven his innocence, which is an idea influenced by Mosaic Law. If there were no witnesses to the crime, God determined whether the accused was guilty or not through some sort of test, for example, through *järnbörden*, where the accused could prove his innocence by carrying burning irons in his arms.

When the first laws were written, the state achieved greater importance as an official power, for example, by granting rights and better living conditions to women, regardless of whether or not their husbands or families approved of these changes. One such right was the right to inheritance. Whereas in the Early Middle Age, women could only inherit their family's estate if there was no male heir, in the middle of the thirteenth century, women's right to inheritance increased, and by law they could now inherit half as much as their brothers.

Sweden's oldest written law is Äldre Västgötalagen from around the year 1220. The oldest existing copy of the full law is from 1280. This text is also the oldest book written in the Swedish language. The writing of a uniform law for the country became one of the main forces to create a centralized system of power.

FOREIGN INFLUENCE ON LANGUAGE

During the Viking Age, trade had flourished, and many modern towns bear the names of *köping* (trade), for example, Norrköping, Linköping, Jönköping, Köpinge. When Sweden became Christianized, the older trading posts, such as Birka, were abandoned, and newer towns were built. Many of these were placed a bit inland rather than by the coasts, perhaps in an attempt to avoid attacks by pirates and plunderers of the sea. While the Vikings traveled the world and took their trade to foreign countries in the Early Middle Age, Sweden was heavily influenced by the Hanseatic League and the German merchants in trade, politics, and growth of cities and merchant colonies. Many towns were founded as a result of this commercial activity. The city of Visby on the island of Gotland became a flourishing trading post, and one of the largest in the region during the thirteenth century.

The remnants of a fort in Visby, Gotland. The island has many historic sites, including an Early Middle Age ring wall. The great ring wall of Visby, completed around 1288, is about a mile long on the sea side. It protected the city against plunderers.

German words began creeping into the Swedish language. Despite the German influence, Swedish is not so similar to German that a German-speaking person can understand it without training. Norwegian, on the other hand, is very closely related, with only minor differences. Most Swedes can also understand Danish fairly well, and vice versa. Swedish people from different parts of the country speak dialects. For example, Skåne, in southern Sweden, and the island of Gotland have very distinct dialects. The dialects of the people of the north are also easily distinguished from those around the Stockholm area.

Foreigners might find the *sj*-sounds, as used in *sju* (seven), in the Swedish language the most difficult to pronounce. You can think of the *sj*-sound as being similar to *sh* in the English words *ship* or *she*. The *sk*-sound in *skepp* (ship) and *stj*-sound in *stjärna* (star) have similar pronunciations. Other difficult sounds are the *tj* in *tjock* (fat) and the *kj* in *kjol* (skirt), and are pronounced similarly to *ch* in *China*. Try this for a tongue twister: *Sju sjösjuka sjömän på ett sjunkande skepp* (seven seasick seamen on a sinking ship).

As people pushed to colonize the north and east across the Baltic to Finland, Sweden grew. Migration from Finland to Sweden and vice versa has been an ongoing process into modern times. In the northern parts of Sweden there is a fairly large population called *Finlands-Svenskar* (Finland-Swedes), who speak both Finnish and Swedish.

BIRGER JARL AND THE FOUNDING OF STOCKHOLM

Birger Jarl was the greatest ruler of Middle Age Sweden and an important figure in Swedish history. Birger Jarl belonged to the Folkung Dynasty, 1250–1363 (*folk-ung*, Folke's young, descendants of Folke Filbyter. There is some debate about whether this ancestor really existed, or if the name Folkung has other origins). The word *jarl* originally meant free man and later took on the meaning of Earl. The jarl was second only to the king in power. He could become the official ruler, since the kings were often weak or appointed at a very young age, perhaps because it was easier to agree on a young boy-king who could then be molded and strengthened under the influence of the nobles. Birger Jarl was the Earl of Sweden in 1250–66, and acted as regent for his underage son Valdemar, who was elected king in the year 1250, when King Erik Eriksson died.

Old Town, with its cobblestone streets, is a popular shopping destination.

Photo: www.imagebank.sweden.se © Preben Kristensen, Stockholm Visitors Board.

Old Town has old buildings and narrow streets, some so narrow that if you stand in the center and extend both arms straight out to your sides, you can touch the buildings on either side.

Storkyrkan (the Big Church), dedicated in 1306, is the oldest building in Gamla Stan.

Birger Jarl worked for the establishment of a strong central government, and for cooperation with the church. Mälaren, the lake which joins the Baltic Sea, was an important and nearly perfect location for a city, and Birger Jarl is credited with the founding of Stockholm, the nation's capital. Stockholm was originally established as a defense outpost on the island that is now Gamla Stan (Old Town), and grew within a hundred years to be the largest settlement in Sweden.

Birger Jarl began the construction of a fort on one of the central islands, where the Royal Palace now stands. He increased trade with the Germans by allowing them to enter Swedish harbors without being taxed. Stockholm became the new chief commercial port and industrial city, later gaining importance as an exporter of metals, timber, and furs, and took over as the capital of Sweden after Birka and Sigtuna.

The center of the city is built on thirteen islands, where Mälaren joins the Baltic Sea, with remnants of the original city in Gamla Stan on three small islands: Stadsholmen, Riddarholmen, and Helgeandsholmen. The islands are close to each other and connected with bridges. Old Town is therefore often referred to as Staden Mellan Broarna (The City Between the Bridges).

The parliament stands on Helgeandsholmen just a few steps from the Royal Palace. Also located here is Medeltidsmuseet (the Middle Age Museum), which was built in the late 1970s when a construction crew working on a parking garage underneath the parliament ran into a Swedish Middle Age stonewall, now located in the center of the museum in its original place. During excavations, several objects and artifacts were recovered, and it was decided that construction on the parking garage be abandoned and the place be made into a museum.

Birger Jarl continued ruling until his death, when his son Valdemar became king. In a dispute in 1275, with the help of a mostly Danish army, Birger Jarl's second son, Magnus Birgersson "Ladulås" defeated Valdemar's Swedish army. Valdemar was captured, but later freed and made Duke of Götalandskapen. It is speculated that Magnus Ladulås (barn-lock) got his name because he established a law that prevented the nobility from forcibly visiting and taking advantage of the farmers. In other words, he "locked the barn."

The City Hall viewed from across the water. The City Hall was built between 1911 and 1923 and inaugurated in 1923, four hundred years after the entry into Stockholm of Gustav Vasa, the founder of the Swedish National State.

The City Hall's Golden Hall, covered with glass and gold mosaic.
Photo: www.imagebank.sweden.se © E. Dennis, Stockholm Visitors Board.

This golden coffin at the base of the tower of City Hall in Stockholm is a monument to Birger Jarl. In reality, Birger Jarl is buried in Varnhems Klosterkyrka in Västergötland. His tomb was opened in 2002 and the remains identified and confirmed to be his.

Chapter Five
Late Middle Age: 1300–1500

OVERVIEW

Sweden, in its Late Middle Age, was characterized by struggles between church and state, between the farmers and the *frälse* (a tax-exempt privileged nobility), and among royal brothers. It is therefore necessary to give a quick overview before digging into the specifics of this time period.

When the *stormän* observed the king getting richer through taxation of the farmers, they thought their current wealth insufficient. Fights erupted, the *stormän* attempting to overthrow the king. These conflicts led to one revolution after another, often fought with hired foreign soldiers at great expense. In order to fund the wars, the king increased the tax burden on the farmers, but was eventually forced to borrow money from foreign nobles and give his forts as collateral. Several Swedish forts ended up in Danish and German ownership, with the taxes from the supporting provinces going directly to the foreigners.

Farmers who tried to hide their savings or cattle from the king were imprisoned, but might regain their freedom by agreeing to sign their farm over to the reigning *storman*. If they refused, they were severely punished, sometimes with mutilation or dismemberment. The *frälse* acquired much previously taxable land, which became non-taxable due to their tax-exempt privilege, making the economic situation in Sweden dire. The poverty had never been worse, and many farmers were forced to become beggars.

With poverty and starvation came diseases such as smallpox and plague, with Digerdöden (the Black Death) peaking in the late 1340s and wiping out one-third of Sweden's population within a year. The farmers were hit the hardest, but nobody was immune. The strongest *stormän* used the opportunity to buy deserted farms in both Sweden and Denmark. One of the most powerful nobles, a man by the name of Bo Johnsson Grip, ended up owning one-fifth of all land in Sweden. This acquisition of so much by so few divided the tax-exempt nobility into the upper and lower *frälse*.

Around 1350, the Folkung Dynasty unified the country by introducing a supreme law covering the entire region. The new centralized government was made possible through increased trade and expansion in mining, and survived on income from the many farms and cooperation between the Nordic countries. The first true cities started to emerge, and with the introduction of new taxes, an even greater portion of the farming fell in the hands of the king, *stormän*, and church. Through donations by rich *stormän*, the church grew in power and became a large owner of land.

In 1397, under the leadership of Queen Margareta, Kalmarunionen (a union between the Nordic countries) became a reality, and the next hundred years were characterized by stiff conflicts between those favoring a monarchy and those favoring a state ruled by the aristocracy. In 1434, when Erik of Pomerania (Queen Margareta's successor to the throne) attempted to realize the aristocratic state, a rebellion led by a man named Engelbrekt Engelbrektsson broke out, resulting in Erik's ouster. Farmers and miners gained greater power and started attending political gatherings, which eventually led to the institution of Riksdagen (the parliament). In 1477, Sweden's first university, with primary lectures in philosophy, law, and theology, was established in Uppsala under the guidance of Archbishop Jacob Ulfsson.

ALBREKT OF MECKLENBURG

In the fourteenth century, the king pawned so much land to foreigners that Svea Rike was falling apart. The Danes and Germans were fighting for the opportunity to reign in Sweden. The farmers and lower *frälse* attempted to defend the country against a foreign takeover. The upper *frälse* rebelled against the king, Magnus Eriksson, and asked for support to conquer Sweden from the German *storman*, Albrekt of Mecklenburg (who was the king's son-in-law and later succeeded to the throne anyway). The upper *frälse* was awarded large lots of land and the right to use the country's many forts. As a result, Sweden lost much of its independence to foreign powers.

The Swedish people were treated brutally by the Germans, who had a strong foothold in Sweden through the Hanseatic League, a powerful merchant association that included eight German towns that cooperated in trade and war within northern Germany and the Baltic. However, the influence of the Germans allowed Sweden's economy to develop to a considerable degree.

The Germans gained substantive power and initiated a law stating that half of the city's council had to be German. The extensive privileges Albrekt of Mecklenburg gave them, along with his attempt to acquire additional land from the nobility, displeased the Swedish people. They soon came to regret their choice of Albrekt as king and subsequently tried to dethrone him. The nobility solicited the help of Queen Margareta of Denmark who, in 1389, put together an army

The smaller state coat of arms of Sweden shows a blue shield with three crowns in gold. It was used as the seal of the Swedish kingdom for the first time in 1364.

Illustration: www.imagebank.sweden.se
© Swedish National Archives.

that defeated King Albrekt's warriors and ended the Mecklenburg rule. Margareta was then recognized as Sweden's reigning queen.

The smaller state coat of arms of Sweden is one of the oldest symbols of Sweden as a nation. The shield with the crowns appears on money, police cars, and in the name of the Swedish national ice hockey team, *Tre Kronor* (Three Crowns). The symbol is so "Swedish" that many Swedes don't reflect on its meaning or age.

There are several theories about the origin of the three crowns. One is that they have religious importance and symbolize the three wise men. However, there is no proof that this theory is valid. Albrekt of Mecklenburg introduced the state arms in his seal in 1364 when he became ruler of Sweden. However, Magnus Eriksson, who was king of Sweden and

Norway in 1332, and who acquired Skåne (in what is now southern Sweden) from the Danish kingdom, also established the three crowns as a symbol, perhaps of the three parts of his kingdom: Sweden, Norway, and Skåne. The three crowns were therefore already a symbol of Sweden when Albrekt of Mecklenburg thirty years later had it engraved in his seal. A third theory is that the crowns represent the three kingdoms of Sweden, Norway, and Denmark during the Union of Kalmar in 1397.

QUEEN MARGARETA AND THE UNION OF KALMAR

Margareta Valdemarsdotter was born in Denmark in 1353 and is noted for her creation of a single kingdom. Margareta became ruler of Sweden, Norway, and Denmark through the Union of Kalmar in 1397.

Swedes, Norwegians, and Danes commonly intermarried in order to strengthen the bonds between the countries, and King Valdemar Attertag of Denmark married off his daughter Margareta to King Håkon of Norway, who was the son of the Swedish king Magnus Eriksson. When both King Valdemar and King Håkon died a few years later, Margareta's and Håkon's son Olav became the rightful heir to the throne of Norway and Denmark. Margareta never officially held the title Queen of Sweden, but since her son was underage, she was appointed as the authorized agent and had reigning power. When Olav died at a young age, Margareta was named "all powerful lady and rightful mistress" of the kingdom, and had the right to rule and choose her successor.

Queen Margareta was a resolute woman with the power and determination to bring together the split Nordic countries. She had learned about politics from her father. Her idea was that if the Nordic countries were united, they could better withstand threats of a hostile takeover from Germany. Her most important mission was to neutralize Germany's threat to acquire Sweden.

Queen Margareta felt that the vast immigration of Germans, along with the Hanseatic League, which dominated the trade in Scandinavia, imposed a threat on the Swedish people and country. She pledged to maintain all of the Swedes' rights, freedoms, and privileges, and to work to restore Sweden's former boundaries. She supported the idea that the Nordic countries should join forces in an effort to end the Hanseatic League's monopoly in the Baltic Sea.

The Nordic Union was officially established in a meeting in Kalmar (located on Sweden's southeastern coast) between the Nordic nobility and the priests in 1397. The Union of Kalmar declared in part that the three kingdoms should have only one king in order to forever preserve the peace between them, and to effect greater power against foreign forces. Kings often ruled over combined kingdoms, more in an effort to preserve local customs and interests than to form a single country. Under the Union of Kalmar, the local laws of the different countries were preserved, with the king governing according to the law of each realm. In terms of international issues, the Nordic countries appeared as one, while in terms of national issues, each country had the right to self-rule. Sweden achieved its longest period of peace during Margareta's reign. She has therefore popularly been referred to as the "Queen of Peace."

The upper warrior class had held much of the real power in Sweden, and it wasn't until later, after the Union of Kalmar, that the monarchy was made hereditary. Since Margareta had no living children of her own, she chose her niece's son, Bogislav, as her successor, changing his name to Erik (Erik of Pomerania), a name she found better suited for a Nordic king.

Erik was recognized as the rightful heir to the kingdom, but Margareta continued ruling until her death in 1412.

Although the Union of Kalmar was an important attempt to eliminate the strong influence of the Germans, both the nobility and the commoners questioned its strength. After Margareta's death, the Swedish people were at odds over whether to preserve the Union or strive for their independence. The Union eventually failed, partially because of Erik's poor ruling power, but also because the Swedish people longed for independence from the other Nordic countries. It was after the Union of Kalmar's collapse in 1523 that Sweden truly started to develop the national identity that we know today.

THE HOLY BIRGITTA

Another noteworthy woman of Middle Age Sweden is the Holy Birgitta, Sweden's most important medieval saint. Born in 1303 to a father who was a mighty *storman* and judge, and a mother who was related to the Folkung Family, Birgitta became, through her parents' and husband's standing, a leading politician in Middle Age Sweden. From childhood, Birgitta was drawn to the idea of becoming a nun, but was married off at the age of thirteen to a man five years her senior. Together they had eight children.

Inwardly, Birgitta struggled between supporting the worldly lifestyle that came with her upbringing, and a longing for a simpler and more secluded life. Birgitta had had several revelations during childhood, which made her feel that she had been chosen by God. After her husband's death in 1344, she started seeing herself as a messenger of God, with a duty to report the contents of her revelations to both political and religious leaders. Her "Heavenly Revelations," about six hundred of them, were collected in a book, which is treasured as one of Sweden's earliest literary works.

> *True humbleness is . . . to walk the road of Jesus . . . not to long*
> *for superfluous abundance, but to be as the common man.*

—The Holy Birgitta

A woman in the Middle Ages generally had little say about the world. Some saw Birgitta as a proud and powerful negotiator who used religion to further her political goals, others saw her as a visionary leader and a true messenger of God. Birgitta spent much of her life traveling throughout Europe. She visited the pope in Rome to seek approval to establish a monastic order for both monks and nuns. She was well educated about the happenings in the world and was probably influenced by the views of both noblemen and church leaders, whom she criticized fearlessly for failing to support the ideals they preached, such as respectful treatment of the poor. She felt that the king's primary duty was as a caretaker of the crown and people, and not the other way around. The Swedish king and the pope listened to Birgitta's messages without criticizing or condemning her.

After a pilgrimage to Jerusalem, Birgitta died in Rome in 1373. Her children brought her remains back to Sweden, and her relics are stored at Vadstena Congregation in middle Sweden. She was canonized in 1391.

ERIK OF POMERANIA

Erik of Pomerania was thirty years old when he became ruler of the Nordic Union. Erik attempted to continue Queen

Saint Birgitta in an engraving by Adrian Collaert that shows a variant
spelling of her name in its caption.

Photo: www.imagebank.sweden.se, engraved by Adrian Collaert, © The Royal
Library, Sweden.

Margareta's policies but lacked the political influence, and life within the Union became burdened with conflicts. His vision was to unify the three nations into one and to control trade in the Baltic Sea. This required breaking the power of the Hanseatic League, which responded by officially blocking all trade to the Nordic countries. Erik in turn established a heavy toll (Öresundstullen) in the strait of Öresund between Sweden and Denmark. The trade blockage led to conflicts with the cities of northern Germany, followed by isolation and starvation for the Swedes. Salt, vital for the preservation of food, became a rarity, and the miners in the city of Bergslagen were unable to export their iron and copper. Unemployment followed.

This constant warfare required greater taxes driven in by the king's bailiffs. Few farmers had the capacity to pay and many were again at risk of losing their properties or becoming forced laborers at the forts. In addition, the shortage of money led to the minting of copper, which devalued Swedish currency and made the situation even worse.

In an effort to turn the Nordic countries into an absolute monarchy and create a citizenry dependent on the king, Erik took up residence in Copenhagen in Denmark, the wealthiest of the Nordic countries. He appointed Danes and Germans who were loyal to him as bailiffs for the forts in Sweden. This deprived the Swedes of jobs and created an upper class that thrived on collecting taxes and had little regard for the welfare of the country and the common man. The king's policies antagonized the broad masses of Swedes, who had just recently rid themselves of Albrekt of Mecklenburg, and their great discontent eventually culminated in the Engelbrekt rebellion in 1434.

THE ENGELBREKT REBELLION

The Engelbrekt rebellion started when farmers and miners in Bergslagen refused to pay taxes. They chose Engelbrekt Engelbrektsson as their leader. Engelbrekt belonged to the lower *frälse* and was a member of a wealthy mining family with military experience against the Hanseatic League. Engelbrekt and his army of more than fifty thousand men set several forts on fire and freed many of the provinces. In August 1434, the most powerful men of the upper *frälse* attended a meeting in which Engelbrekt forced them to write a letter to Erik of Pomerania, demanding a tax reduction and threatening angry masses if it was not granted. In order to gain support and to prove that he intended only to oust the foreign *stormän* from the country, Engelbrekt encouraged the Swedish nobility to occupy the forts that had escaped the fires. The liberation army was divided into three parts. One, under the leadership of the *frälse*, was entrusted with conquering Kalmar Castle, but failed and had to enter into a truce with the occupying force. The other two parts, comprised of farmers, succeeded in gaining control over all of southern Sweden within a month, with the exception of Kalmar.

When the king received the message, he left Denmark for Sweden with a great army and fleet. In the meantime, several provinces united and, under the leadership of Engelbrekt, sent men to surround Stockholm. The king was forced into negotiations where it was decided that for one year no taxes were to be paid to the king. Engelbrekt called together representatives for the farmers, merchants, and priests in Sweden's first Riksdag (parliament), and attempted to convince the upper *frälse* to join in the fight. But the upper *frälse* continued siding with the king in exchange for personal benefits and continued imposing taxes on the farmers. The farmers remained embittered.

In January 1436, a new Riksdag gathered, followed by a new rebellion with armies storming Stockholm. Within a three-month period, Engelbrekt's rebels occupied all forts still in the king's possession. By April 1436, the whole country was in uproar. The farmers' worst enemies were the king's bailiffs. Together with the lower *frälse*, the farmers formed a front, turning over some of the occupied forts to the upper *frälse* in order to win them over. This incentive, given to only some of the elite, split the power of the upper *frälse*, finally allowing the rebels to dispose of the foreign bailiffs. Erik of Pomerania was still seen as the king of Sweden, but in practicality the nobility and Riksdag ruled the country.

In 1436, a longtime enemy assassinated Engelbrekt. After his death, the aristocracy regained control of the country's forts and again united to defeat the farmers. Over a two-year period, the farmers held their ground against the armed troops in several battles and reached some of their most important goals: The tax was decreased by a third, the king's foreign bailiffs were driven from the country, many of the hated forts were burned to the ground, and the parliament was officially established. There the farmers' voices could be heard, allowing them to reach greater political power.

The tax decrease allowed some farmers to return to their abandoned farms, save some of the surplus, and plan for the future. This reprieve, in turn, led to the development of better tools and easier work. The economic upswing demanded more iron and copper for tools and household utensils, catapulting the mining industry to a new high. The use of waterpower allowed the miners to heat the smelters to temperatures high enough to melt the iron. Many of those previously driven from their farms and unable to return to farming now found new and more profitable employment in the mines. From this time to the modern day, Sweden has been known as one of the biggest exporters of iron in the world.

Church door dating to the middle of the fifteenth century. Displayed at the Museum of History in Stockholm.

As a result of better living conditions and greater productivity, trade with foreign countries increased. Ships, mainly from Germany, came to Swedish harbors. The Swedes traded iron, tar, and butter for foreign salt and clothing. The new class structure that emerged was comprised of a *riksföreståndare* (national administrator), followed by the upper *frälse* and the bishop. The church owned about one-fifth of all farms. On the next rung were merchants, miners, the lower *frälse*, and priests, with free farmers and craftsmen below. The lower classes consisted of the working class, those farmers who no longer owned land, only tools and animals, and poorer people seeking employment. At the bottom were the beggars, who had nothing, not even a job.

The Engelbrekt uprising played an important role in the struggle for an independent Sweden. Farmers were better prepared to use their weapons to defend their rights, and the upper nobility was forced to build a strong Swedish state that could withstand and counter wars with foreign powers. The fifteenth century chronicler Ericus Olai pays homage to Engelbrekt as a defender of liberty: "The most valiant, brave, and loyal man . . . always ready to die for the inhabitants of the Swedish kingdom." Despite the relatively short time period in which Engelbrekt Engelbrektsson led his army against the king and his bailiffs, he is seen as a hero who originated the people's liberation from the tyrannical monarchy and is one of the few Middle Age personalities still alive in the soul of the Swedish people.

THE BATTLE OF BRUNKENBERG

The Nordic countries embraced different languages and institutions, and had difficulties agreeing on where sovereignty should lie. For example, Denmark had a strong tradition of royal authority, while Sweden was ruled by the higher aristocracy and the church, and gave their king only limited power. Some of the problems the countries faced were: Should they embrace a monarchy or an aristocratic state? Should they operate under a feudal system or avoid it? What if somebody owned land in more than one country? Different ideas about the character of the state divided the people of the Nordic Union and led to conflicts.

The Battle of Brunkenberg in October 1471 is seen as a turning point in Swedish history. Sten Sture the Elder, the personal executor of the former king Karl Knutsson (who succeeded Erik of Pomerania and King Kristofer of Bavaria), was ruling in Sweden when King Kristian I of Denmark proclaimed himself king of the country and arrived in Stockholm to reclaim the Royal Palace and his kingdom. The core of the conflict lay in the fact that the king of the Nordic Union was Danish. He could therefore draw strength from his homeland, but he lacked the support of the Swedes who longed for their independence.

In a deciding battle that culminated on the Brunkenberg ridge in Stockholm, Sten Sture clashed with the pro-Union Kristian I. Merchants, farmers, and *stormän* with interests in international trade and mining supported Sten Sture. King Kristian I fought with the Danes on his side, in addition to certain nobility and peasantry from Uppland in middle Sweden (although most Swedish nobility fought not for their country but for their personal interests). The battle was fierce with an estimated combined two thousand casualties. The victory at the Brunkenberg ridge led to a national awakening, with Sten Sture at the helm: the law stating that half of the city's council had to be German was repealed, foreigners could no longer hold official positions in Sweden, and the Union of Kalmar lost much of its power and was dissolved in 1523.

Despite his lack of royal lineage, Sten Sture held political power in Sweden for almost three decades and laid much of the groundwork for Sweden's independence from the other Nordic countries. He focused on the declaration that Sweden was a free realm, that Sweden should be governed in accordance with the principle that what concerned the people should be agreed upon by the people, with all rules requiring the consent of the common man.

Sten Sture the Elder died in 1503 and was succeeded by Hans Johan II, Svante Nilsson Sture, and later Sten Sture the Younger. The struggle for an independent Sweden would culminate through Sten Sture the Younger's efforts, in the event known as Stockholm's Bloodbath.

STOCKHOLM'S BLOODBATH

Stockholm's Bloodbath is the name of a series of executions that took place on Stortorget (the grand market square) in Stockholm in November 1520, following the crowning of King Kristian II in Storkyrkan (the Big Church) there. Eighty-two men who had fought against Kristian II prior to his crowning were beheaded, despite having been given unrestricted amnesty in writing. The Bloodbath was the revenge of Archbishop Gustav Trolle for the confiscation of his title and land by opposing forces prior to the king's crowning.

Toward the end of its Middle Age, Sweden was a split kingdom. On one side were those who stood for a unified North, the Vasa, Oxenstierna, and Trolle clans, with the archbishop as the leading man. On the other were those who stood for an independent Sweden, the Bonde and Sture clans, who found a leader in Sten Sture the Younger. Much of the conflict was about political and economic power, rather than patriotism or sentimental national interests.

The struggle between church and state was coming to a head when Sten Sture the Younger accused Archbishop Gustav Trolle of conspiracy to crown the Danish king Kristian II king of Sweden. In a parliamentary meeting in 1517, representatives of the Sture clan decided that Gustav Trolle should be removed from his position and his castle Stäket demolished. Kristian invaded Sweden to reclaim and protect Stäket. Gustav Trolle was at the time the underdog in the conflict and imprisoned in spite of Kristian II's support. Later, the revenge hungry Trolle would have his chance to act on the crimes the people had committed against him.

In early January 1520, Sten Sture the Younger was fatally wounded in battle, and Kristian II laid Stockholm under siege. Stockholm eventually surrendered. When Archbishop Trolle crowned Kristian II king of Sweden, he did so on the condition that the new king should protect the church. King Kristian II promised to rule according to Swedish custom, to forgive the past, to respect the rights of those defeated, to protect the church and the defenseless, and to require all to follow the established law. However, when the three-day crowning feast ended, Archbishop Trolle stepped forward as executive agent for the Union. He read his accusations against the Sture clan and those who had confiscated his land and removed him from power, and reminded the new king of what he had promised regarding law and order and the protection of the church.

When the accusations were read, Sten Sture the Younger's widow, Kristina Gyllenstierna, who had attempted to defend Stockholm and the Royal Palace Tre Kronor (Three Crowns) after her husband's death, pointed out that Gustav Trolle had been removed from his position in 1517 by the people. Many isolated individuals, as well as larger groups from the whole country, had together decided to remove the archbishop from his position and destroy his castle. The people had sworn to ward off all legal consequences or papal judgments regarding the matter. In addition, she pointed out that those few who had carried out the act of removing Trolle had acted on behalf of the people and should not be punished for the combined decision of the masses, and that the archbishop had been present to witness the meeting.

The new king, Kristian II, had reinstated Trolle as archbishop. Legal proceedings followed, led by Trolle and a clerical court comprised of fourteen of the Swedish Church's most prominent men. It was decided that rules agreed upon by heretics were invalid and that the punishment for heresy was death. The amnesty the king had granted Sten Sture's people was invalid. Ultimately, the church had control over such matters, but the king was left with the burden of carrying out the judgment, and doing so immediately. King Kristian II is therefore the one most often remembered and hated figures of the episode called Stockholm's Bloodbath.

When the judgment was read, the gates to the Royal Palace in Stockholm were closed to prevent escape until the king had time to consider the punishment. Arrests followed, and by order of the king, the court met on November 8, 1520 at the Royal Palace and brought forth the executions on November 8 and 9, after which the bodies were burned in a great pyre. Those executed included two bishops and several nobles with their servants. The body of Sten Sture the Younger was dug up from its grave to be burned with the other bodies.

Kristina Gyllenstierna and other noble ladies escaped death. Instead of being executed in Sweden, they were imprisoned in Denmark. Gyllenstierna survived her imprisonment and later returned to Stockholm. King Kristian II went back to Denmark where he was celebrated as a hero by the Danes and acquired the nickname Kristian Bondekär (he who loves the farmer). In Sweden, he became known as Kristian Tyrann (the tyrant).

Stortorget, the site of Stockholm's Bloodbath, as it looks today.

Gustav Trolle might have felt that now, with the nationalist leadership eliminated, the call for an independent Sweden would be silenced. But the ideals of national freedom die hard. Almost a century prior to Stockholm's Bloodbath, Bishop Thomas of Strängnäs, who was against the Danish leadership and the Nordic Union, expressed in his famous 1439 poem *Frihetsvisan* (Song of Freedom) as a tribute to Engelbrekt Engelbrektsson:

> *Frihet är det bästa ting, där sökas kan all världen omkring . . .*
> *du älska frihet mer än guld . . .* (Freedom is the finest thing,
> one can seek in this world . . . you treasure freedom more
> than gold . . .)

101

Stockholm's Bloodbath should not be seen as an isolated event. Rather, it was the culmination of a long and bitter struggle between a split people embracing two different schools of thought. Stockholm's Bloodbath was a desperate attempt to defend the obsolete union between Sweden, Norway, and Denmark instituted by Queen Margareta in 1397. The Union of Kalmar was intended to foster cooperation and loyalty between the Nordic countries, but when the leadership the Union so desperately needed died with Queen Margareta, the Danish king started to see the interests of the Danes as primary, which alienated the Swedes. Stockholm's Bloodbath provoked a new rebellion, which a year later led the Swedish nobleman Gustav Vasa to seize power. He was soon elected king of Sweden.

Chapter Six
Vasa Age: 1500–1700

GUSTAV VASA

Stockholm's Bloodbath was the event that ignited the liberation war of 1521–23. Also called the Vasa rebellion, it was led by Gustav Vasa, a nobleman who managed to secure Sweden's independence from the Danes and the Union of Kalmar.

Gustav Vasa belonged to one of the mightiest families of the time. The Vasa clan was originally allied with the Danes, but there were also generations of Vasas who had been on both sides of the Union conflict. Gustav Eriksson Vasa became a follower of Sten Sture the Younger.

Gustav Vasa's father was one of the nobles executed in the Bloodbath, and many of his relatives were put in prison. This strike against his family brought Gustav Vasa to the brink of financial ruin. He himself was taken prisoner in Denmark, but when he heard of the attacks against the Swedes, he escaped and put together an army of several thousand men, whom he convinced to prepare to die in battle for the ideal of an independent Sweden.

Since Gustav Vasa was a prison escapee, he had to dress like a peasant to conceal his identity. In November 1520, he arrived in Dalarna (the core province of the Sture resistance north of Stockholm, which held the chief idea of emancipation from the Union of Kalmar), with a plan to recruit forces from the free and armed farmers who lived there. When he failed to gain their support, he continued on skis toward

Picture of Gustav Vasa, displayed at Stockholm City Museum in Sweden.

Norway. Right at this time, news of Stockholm's Bloodbath reached Dalarna and angered the people. The city's two best skiers set out to track Vasa down, convince him to return to Dalarna, and lead in their struggle against king Kristian Tyrann of Denmark. In January 1521, the people of Dalarna elected Gustav Vasa their leader and allowed the liberation war to begin.

(This landmark event is still celebrated. Four hundred years later, in 1922, a ninety-kilometer race on skis, called Vasa-loppet, was instituted in memory of Gustav Vasa's flight and the race to catch him and bring him back to Dalarna. Vasa-loppet has become a national tradition, with thousands of participants each year. The motto, *"I fäders spår för framtids segrar,"* which means "In our forefathers' footprints for future victories," was composed in 1923 and mounted at the finish line. The city of Mora in Minnesota—a sister city to the Swedish Mora, with a population of approximately 3200—holds a Vasa-lopp ski-race each year to commemorate the event and the many Swedish immigrants who live in Minnesota.)

Gustav Vasa's first move as the leader of the rebellion was to ask for weapons and manpower from the German city of Lübeck. Since the Danish king Kristian II was planning to drive the Lübeck traders away from Scandinavian waters, Lübeck had no problem supporting the Vasa rebellion and lent him military support in return for trade privileges, such as freeing Lübeck from customs duties and taxes, and giving its citizens exclusive right to trade in Sweden for all time. This agreement on monopoly was, of course, a bit extreme and not possible to uphold for centuries to come. But that was a problem Gustav Vasa would deal with later.

With Lübeck's assistance, Gustav Vasa's army increased the pressure on the forts and conquered one city at a time. The rebellion spread south and east to the Baltic Sea. In 1522, several cities had been conquered, but Stockholm and Kalmar were still under Danish control. The following summer, Gustav Vasa conquered the last of the castles controlled by the Danes. He was elected king of Sweden on June 6, 1523, a date that has remained Sweden's National Holiday and is honored as a reminder of Sweden's independence from Denmark and the Union of Kalmar.

Although Gustav Vasa had little experience ruling a country, he set the lofty goal of freeing Sweden from its poverty and building a rich and independent nation, strong enough to withstand wars with foreign powers. He reasoned that a king who is part of the people, who understands their issues, and who rules from within is difficult to dethrone. He felt that in order to be effective, a ruler must live within the country he rules and not in some other far away place, as had been the case with the Danish kings. Despite the fact that the people, after the war, slipped back to their discontent with the state's demands for higher taxes, Gustav Vasa is credited as the person responsible for laying a sound foundation for the Swedish National State.

Following the war with the Danes, Gustav Vasa was again broke. The biggest problem was the huge war debt, which, in 1526, had only been paid by about a third. Vasa began thinking about how to obtain money and build up a reserve for the future. He installed tolls on foreign trade and encouraged the mining of silver and the minting of money. He invested in Swedish mines, turning mining into a large industry. He supervised his bailiffs and made sure the state's income and expenses were recorded. He enforced the *frälse's* duty to supply the king with armed soldiers to strengthen the army. Gustav Vasa became one of the richest kings in the history of Sweden.

In order to further strengthen his position, Gustav Vasa quickly took advantage of the new teachings of Olaus Petri (whose original name was Olof Persson), a clergyman and a zealous reformer of the Swedish Church. Olaus Petri challenged the old ways of thinking. He stood at the forefront of the religious reformation and is credited with shaping much of Sweden's religious phase. Throughout the first years of the reformation, Olaus Petri handed out several Protestant writings, among them a Swedish translation of the New Testament. Gustav Vasa made good use of many of the teachings, for example, the relationship between the king and the people, which stated that the king was God's representative with the responsibility to carry out God's will, to serve the people, and to promote the welfare of the common man. The state's primary responsibility was to guard over the people's moral and religious upbringing through education.

Gustav Vasa started the religious reformation through the parliament meeting in Västerås in 1527. His goal was not necessarily to convert Sweden to the Protestant faith, but rather to get rid of competing powers, to subordinate the Church to the state, and to establish supremacy of the state through the monarch. The Lutheran Church denied the authority of the pope as a foreign superior and supported the crown's right to draw from the Church's resources. This affirmation suited Gustav Vasa well. The farmers still rebelled against the upper nobility and the unfair taxation, so Gustav Vasa decided that it was the Church's duty to resolve the problem with the economy. He suggested that the wealth of the Church really belonged to the people and required that a large part of the Church's estates revert back to the state. The Church owned huge swaths of real estate, and the reduction of the Church's land gave Sweden a more permanent economic backing. The reduction of the Church's land also decreased the Church's power, making it less threatening to the state and giving the state outstanding strength in comparison to the nobility and clergy.

Up until now, the *stormän* had in practicality ruled Sweden and personally benefited from the taxes paid by the common man. Gustav Vasa realized that this exploitation of the people must end. He divided the larger provinces into smaller territories, and instead of making the upper class nobility responsible for the provinces, he hired less noble *fogdar* (bailiffs), who were loyal to the king and reported to him directly. Vasa's control over local territories meant that the economic interests of the state could be satisfied more easily. Law and order were upheld and farming was nourished. His decision, in 1544, to make the crown hereditary was a move intended to end the *stormän's* exploitation of Sweden's money and resources, and to secure power for the future. However, after Vasa's reign and toward the end of the sixteenth century, the privileges of the big man's class were also made hereditary, and the nobility received more benefits, such as priority over the common man to hold important political posts and offices, exemption from tax and tolls on trade, release from paying all new taxes, and exclusive rights to hunt and fish on the land surrounding their farms. At court, only nobles were granted the privilege to judge other nobles. These changes reduced the power of the parliament to a select few. In practicality, Sweden was again ruled by the upper nobility and those closest to the king, which amounted to the twenty or so richest families in the country.

Gustav Vasa was considered the first king to rule over an independent Sweden. Although he is often credited as being a man of the people, the truthfulness and practicality of this statement can be debated. It is important to note the recurrent pattern of privileges given to the upper nobility and the Church, at the expense of higher taxes imposed on the common man. Gustav Vasa had a reputation for being a ruthless king who struck fear in his contemporaries' hearts. He knew just how much to cooperate with his former enemies in order to profit from their relationships. He enlarged the army and built more castles to improve the national defense, but

Sweden has had five dynasties since the monarchy
was made hereditary in 1544: Vasa, Pfalz, Hessen,
Holstein-Gottorp, and Bernadotte, the current dynasty.
The Vasa dynasty's first known member was Nils Ket-
tilsson who lived in the fourteenth century. The name
Vasa was acquired in the 1500s from the family's coat-
of-arms, a vase, a sheaf of corn in gold on top three
slanted fields in blue, silver, and red.

made a serious effort to avoid war. He recruited foreign officials from Germany to help him run the country, yet insisted that the crown remain hereditary. He finally broke the power of the Hanseatic League. He preferred peace to warfare, and he brought Sweden step-by-step closer to becoming a sovereign nation. Twenty years after his crowning, he had achieved a rather advanced administration and had started Sweden on the road toward national strength.

Although the Vasa period was, like so many others, filled with struggles and disputes, where the crushing of one revolt stimulated another (Gustav Vasa managed to dampen several rebellions, among them the Nils Dacke rebellion, which was probably the largest revolt of this time), Gustav Vasa finalized what had started a hundred years earlier as Engelbrekt Engelbrektsson's struggle for freedom, and Vasa's appeals to the farmers left much of the upper nobility powerless. Vasa's primary contributions to Swedish history include Sweden's emancipation from the Union of Kalmar and the Catholic Church, and the strengthening of the state's economy. His founding of the Swedish National State led, in the following century, to Sweden's Age of Greatness. Gustav Vasa ruled until his death in 1560, but the Vasa Dynasty remained in power for 133 years, from 1521 until 1654.

BRIEF CHURCH HISTORY

In order to grow the economy and fund defense without having to raise taxes, Gustav Vasa decided that Sweden should leave the Catholic Church and become a Protestant country. The religious reformation, which many saw as a "bettering" of the church, started in 1517 when Martin Luther protested against the indulgences of the Catholic Church. The Catholic Church owned one-fifth of all land in Sweden and collected tithe besides, and those who had money could buy a letter of agreement from the church through which they received forgiveness from their sins. In addition, the church services were conducted in Greek or Latin, which the majority of the people could not understand. Martin Luther claimed the Bible carried authority over and above the pope's. During the reformation land and farms previously owned by the church reverted back to the state, and the Swedish king became himself the head of the church, keeping much of the tithe for the state. The Rome-dominated church was transformed into a strictly Swedish institution. This reformation did not just impact the Swedish people's spiritual development, but also their ability to strengthen the Swedish state. Through Gustav Vasa's leadership an effective National State ruled by a central government was established.

The first version of the New Testament in Swedish was published in 1526. In 1541, the entire Bible, called the Gustav Vasa Bible, was published in Swedish. But the reformation was a slow process. The kings were not theologically concerned Lutherans, but used the faith mainly to strengthen the state's position. Differences in opinion between the kings and leaders of this time forced the people to do their own thinking before deciding what was right. As the people's mindset was swayed toward national independence, they also agreed that the Lutheran faith generally fit with their beliefs. The Evangelical Lutheran Swedish Church was officially established in a meeting in Uppsala in 1593, a decision that may have been finalized because of King Sigismund's threat to convert Sweden back to Catholicism. At this point, all Swedish citizens, including children born to at least one parent who was a member of the church, automatically became members.

For the next 250 years, Swedish citizenship and church membership were intertwined. Then, in 1855, the requirement for public affirmation of faith was abolished. In 1951, a law that granted people complete religious freedom was passed, and members of the state were allowed to submit their resignations from the church. Now Swedes become members through baptism rather than birth.

Today, Sweden is divided into thirteen dioceses, each led by a bishop, with the archbishop in Uppsala at the top. The church's highest meeting, where internal questions are discussed and decided upon, is held each August. One such question involves gender: Women attained the right to the priesthood in 1959. This issue has been debated again several times by the heads of the church, but to no avail. Since the Swedish Church is a state church without its own legislative power, the archbishop lacks veto power. The state grants the right and, although the heads of the church don't agree, they and the archbishop have no power to change the decision. The right of women to attain the priesthood was granted alongside the right of male priests to abstain from working with female priests. In 1982, this act was replaced with an act of equal opportunity between men and women, which also applied to the church. Every minister who applies for employment must declare that he or she is prepared to work with ministers of the opposite sex. The first female bishop was ordained in 1997.

Svenska Kyrkan (the Swedish Church) has belonged to the state for several hundred years. The organization of the church became more stable in the seventeenth century, and the church became responsible for the national census. In 1990, this responsibility was handed over to the local tax administration, and today the church is only responsible for recording baptisms, confirmations, church marriages, and the like. On January 1, 2000, the church and state were separated. The Swedish Church now stands on equal terms with other denominations.

Järfälla Kyrka in the author's hometown. The original church was built toward the end of the twelfth century. The main building is from the fifteenth century.

Today, Sweden is one of the most secular countries in the world. The scientific spirit of the Swedish people has lessened their dependence on religion, and most embrace the idea church as part of society, with the primary focus on culture rather than religion. Religious rituals, such as baptisms, confirmations, weddings, and funerals are tradition, but a very small number of the population participates in ordinary mass. A standing joke among today's Swedes is that they go to church twice a year, Easter and Christmas, whether they need to or not.

The churches in Stockholm and most other cities are open at all times between services, so that those who desire to do so can go inside and sit in meditation or prayer. There is usually somebody playing the organ. One of the main differences the author finds between the Swedish and American churches is that Swedish people don't socialize when going to church. Since so few people attend regular services, you seldom know others or meet the same people twice. Also, you come as you are; you don't dress up. For example, most people wear long pants, either dress slacks or blue jeans, when attending mass, but it is fully acceptable to wear cut off jeans, tank top, and flip-flops, if you so desire.

THE DACKE REBELLION

Around the year 1540, the state was so strong that the upper nobility could attack the farmers and drive through another tax increase. At this time, the whole system of taxation was revamped. Rather than paying a common lump sum, with the farmers agreeing amongst themselves how much each should pay, the state recorded all the resources and required each farmer to pay according to the size of his property. This new arrangement allowed the state to tax the people as heavily as possible and resulted in some farmers paying more than others. The differences in taxation split the farmers, making it more difficult for them to unite against further increases.

The discontent among the people sparked the Dacke Rebellion in southern Sweden. In the summer of 1542, a farmer by the name of Nils Dacke led an uprising against *fogdar* and *stormän*, and made several attempts to poison and kill King Gustav Vasa. The king's troops were met with heavy resistance. Thousands of farmers joined in the rebellion, hiding in the thick forests, where they were mobile and attacked without warning. The king's heavily armed troops were unable to operate efficiently. The uprising spread across the country, until the farmers in the south didn't pay any tax at all. The king's army could not feel safe anywhere, and Gustav Vasa was forced into a truce.

Gustav Vasa ordered the castles and forts around the country to strengthen their defense. He expressed contempt for the hired German mercenary soldiers, who so easily fell prey to the peasant army, and he used the truce to accuse the farmers in the south of lacking solidarity when demanding lower taxes. In order to split the farmers, Vasa halted the export of salt and other necessities to the southern provinces, and redirected it to those provinces that were more cooperative. To make matters worse, he also approved a tax reduction for the cooperative provinces. Sweden is a kingdom, he stated, that is to be ruled by the king and not by priests and bishops, as in the old days.

In order to strengthen his troops, Gustav Vasa called upon the *stormän* and hired great numbers of German mercenary soldiers. When he broke the truce, he was able to counter the farmers with a much larger and stronger army. In the winter of 1543, Vasa entered the south with three large armies. He was met with heavy resistance from Nils Dacke's army, but was able to lure the farmers into open terrain. There they lacked the protection of the forest and became easy prey to the hired German elite troops. The farmers suffered heavy losses. In March 1543, Nils Dacke was severely wounded and his men carried him into hiding. In July of that year, Vasa's men found Dacke's hiding place, killed Dacke, chopped his body to pieces, and mounted his head, exposed for all to see, atop a pole in Kalmar. Nils Dacke's many supporters were persecuted.

Although the uprising ended in great loss for the farmers, who were forced to return to a time of oppression, Nils Dacke is considered a hero of the time. He was a simple farmer, fighting for self-government and the freedom of the common man, and against the oppression by the king and what many felt was an idealistic idea of a centrally controlled government. Dacke's *allmogearme* (peasant army), which was comprised of

Smålänningar, Östgötar, and Ölänningar, mainly from the southern part of Sweden, was fighting mostly with crossbows and axes. Despite his loss, Nils Dacke is remembered for his strength, courage, intelligence, and organizational ability. As a strategist, he showed the country the military capability of its poorer and less educated men. And, in the end, Gustav Vasa learned from the Dacke Rebellion. He listened to the complaints of the farmers, did his utmost to get them to accept his policies, and lightened the heavy tax burden.

GUSTAV VASA'S SONS

When the monarchy was made hereditary, the natural progression was for the oldest son to inherit the throne. Gustav Vasa had four sons: Erik, Johan, Magnus, and Karl, with Erik being the oldest and born to Vasa's first wife Katarina. The other three sons were born to Vasa's second wife, Margareta Leijonhufvud. The marriage to Margareta also brought him seven daughters.

Erik was born in 1533 and inherited the kingdom in 1560 when Gustav Vasa died. Vasa's decision to give Erik's younger brothers estates in Finland and Sweden may have helped lay the foundation for a strong family dynasty with significant power against the nobility, but may also have triggered the coming struggles between the brothers.

Gustav Vasa's relatively peaceful reign ended with Erik's vision to strengthen the monarchy by limiting the power of the nobility. This move naturally led to conflicts. Erik also worked to build a strong army employing mercenary troops. The urge to expand the territories was a dominant mark of all of Gustav Vasa's sons. Strategic interests played a vital role, and Erik's foreign policies included an attempt to control the Baltic ports and Russian trade. With Sweden sandwiched between Norway and Denmark to one side and Russia to the

Jakob's Kyrka was built during Johan III's reign and is considered one of Sweden's most beautiful churches.

other, there was fear of being at the mercy of these and other Baltic nations. To quiet this anxiety, Sweden went to war with several countries, including Denmark and Estonia. Estonia's surrender to Sweden in 1561 moved Erik a step closer to his visionary kingdom with control of all of the Baltic.

Erik made several enemies because of his foreign policies and constantly had to be on his guard. He is also said to have been mentally ill. He was overly suspicious and killed those he feared were planning to overthrow him, including several members of the Sture clan. Erik was also suspicious of his own younger brother, Johan. In 1568, Johan and the Sture clan joined forces and took Erik prisoner, which allowed Johan to inherit the crown. It is said that Erik was sent from one prison to another for several years and finally died in prison, from eating poisoned soup.

When Johan became king, his wife Katarina of Poland, who was of the Catholic faith, persuaded Johan to try to reconcile with the Catholic Church. Later, Johan and Katarina's son, Sigismund, was crowned king of Poland. Upon Johan's death in 1592, Sigismund ruled in both Sweden and Poland. When Gustav Vasa's youngest son, Karl, inherited the throne, he expressed his opposition to Catholics and forbid all Catholic Church services in Sweden. This prohibition led to war between Sweden and Catholic Poland. Karl prevailed, but strained his relationship with the nobility considerably.

Karl married Kristina of Holstein-Gottorp, who bore him three children, with the oldest son, Gustav II Adolf, in line for the Swedish throne. Gustav II Adolf was a strong king who managed to lift Sweden into its age of greatness.

AXEL OXENSTIERNA AND SWEDEN'S AGE OF GREATNESS

The seventeenth century is known as Sweden's Age of Greatness. Gustav II Adolf, who inherited the throne when his father Karl IX died in war with Denmark, was crowned king of Sweden in 1611 at the tender age of not-quite-seventeen. Axel Oxenstierna, a councilor of the Swedish state, was chosen legal guardian for the young king. Oxenstierna, who had studied at several German universities and was well learned in politics and world issues, proceeded to educate the king and consult him on military matters. The relationship was mutually beneficial. Oxenstierna's education, courage, insight, and hard work were a good match for the king's natural talent and drive.

As a youngster, Gustav II Adolf was schooled in modern war strategies and politics. His good relations with the aristocracy stabilized the country. He modernized the existing army and is credited with the founding of Göteborg, Sweden's second largest city. At this time, Sweden had a well-managed economy, and a growing mining and weapons industry. In addition, weak economies and unstable political situations in Russia and other European countries contributed to Sweden's success. Gustav II Adolf turned Sweden into a great economic power before his untimely death on a battlefield in Lützen in 1632. He is remembered as one of the most famous of the Swedish kings.

At the termination of the Hanseatic League's power in the Baltic Sea, Sweden was left to compete with other countries over control of the Baltic and coastal regions, and the country was involved in constant warfare. Due to English control of the northern trade route to Russia, Sweden had to focus on trying to establish control over Scandinavia's coastal regions. If Sweden were able to control the trade, harbors, and coastal cities around the Baltic, the Swedish state could also benefit from tolls on foreign traders. When Sweden conquered northern Estonia, it hoped to expand trade farther into the foreign market, but their presence also led to conflicts with Russia, Poland, and Denmark. Those wars had costly consequences but they also required a modernization of the military, which laid the foundation for Sweden's modern compulsory military service. Sweden became one of the first modern European nations with a native standing army in peacetime.

When Gustav II Adolf died in 1632, Axel Oxenstierna became Sweden's foremost statesman. He continued ruling for the next eight years, while acting as the legal guardian for the king's underage daughter Kristina. Oxenstierna gained control over territories in Sweden, Finland, and the Baltic states. After his eight-year reign, disputes with Queen Kristina led to a decline in his power.

THE ROYAL SHIP VASA

As Sweden was modernized and the administration became more advanced, the need to improve its armed forces became evident. Without a strong military, Sweden could not compete or play a vital role throughout the rest of Europe. The army was already fairly efficient, but the navy needed reorganization. Because of poor range and accuracy of the cannons, ships had to confront each other at close range. Several of Sweden's newly acquired ships had been lost, not only in battle, but also due to stormy conditions at sea. Around 1620, the navy consisted of approximately a hundred smaller vessels. The importance of protecting ports around the Baltic Sea created a need to build a number of larger warships.

In 1625, Sweden contracted with a Dutch shipbuilder, who lived in Stockholm, to build four new warships. One of the larger ships was named *Vasa* after the Vasa dynasty. The royal ship was built of oak from the Swedish forest, measured sixty-nine meters in length, and was armed with sixty-four guns. The ship was completed in 1628.

The crew of the *Vasa* had to get used to the rough life at sea and living aboard a ship for many months at a time. Rules were strict on board. The crew slept directly on the wooden deck and lived mainly on grain, peas, and dried meat and fish, with plenty of beer to wash down the heavily salted meat. The ship could carry a total crew of 445 men, including 145 seamen and 300 soldiers. However, its much hoped for success was not to be.

The *Vasa* capsized on her maiden voyage in 1628 and sank to a depth of thirty meters. It has been reported that the main mast, which was fifty-two meters high, could be seen above the water line for many years after the capsize. At the time, the *Vasa* carried a crew of approximately 150 people, with 30–50 men drowning in the accident. It was later determined

The upper deck of the Vasa, *displayed at the Vasa Museum in Stockholm.*

Figurines from the stern of the Vasa. *Note the Vasa coat of arms with the sheaf of corn. Displayed at the Vasa Museum in Stockholm.*

that the ship capsized because it was top heavy and could safely withstand a breeze of only four meters per second. Several tons of stones were stored as ballast, but it was not enough to counter the weight of the guns, masts, and sails.

The royal ship was forgotten and rediscovered in 1956 by a shipwrecking specialist named Anders Franzen. The *Vasa* was raised in 1961, 333 years after she capsized, and in amazingly good shape. The ship was placed in a dry dock, where it was cleaned of mud. Items such as cutlery, tools, and clothing, plus several human skeletons were collected. The ship was conserved and restored to near original condition, with the work completed in 1990. The *Vasa* is the world's best-preserved battleship, and can be viewed at the Vasa Museum in Stockholm.

THE THIRTY YEARS' WAR

The reorganized military, a strong and well-equipped Swedish army and fleet, soon embarked on a journey that would help Sweden acquire large territories along the Baltic coast. The nobility was dissatisfied with their current status and desired to increase their wealth at the expense of foreign countries. The upper nobility helped pull Sweden into the Thirty Years' War (1618–48), which was fought between the many smaller states in central Europe. Sweden entered the war in 1630, when Gustav II Adolf landed twenty-six thousand troops in Germany.

The Thirty Years' War involved a series of military conflicts that were confined primarily to Germany and central Europe. Political goals were often intertwined with religious ones: The Catholic Church's struggle against the Reformation had already led to conflicts and brutal battles in the name of religion, especially in Germany. The Protestant states' desire to control the clergy in order to strengthen their own power over their particular interests, along with territorial conflicts, were tied together with the religious conflicts of the time. The Protestant states were sometimes supportive of the religious faith, and sometimes used it to further their own interests. The neighboring countries were eventually tempted to join the conflict and expanded the war to include a large part of Europe.

In 1630, Gustav II Adolf landed on the European continent to fight for Sweden's status as a defender of Protestants. But the war led to starvation and disease for the farmers. When the army was unable to recruit enough soldiers, it hired from foreign countries. Soon, four-fifths of the Swedish army was made up of foreigners. The soldiers, who were starving as well, plundered the local residents of the different European nations, driving the people from their homes and setting the empty villages on fire.

The Swedish economy was fully focused on supporting the war, but the centuries-old law stating that the nobility had to provide the state with armed soldiers was almost forgotten, and foreign mercenaries, including Germans and Scots, were used in large numbers. In order to fund the war, Sweden gave foreign traders the right to use Swedish mines, forests, and waterpower in return for manufacturing copper and iron for weapons. The Swedish miners were driven from their mines and rivers, and efficient craftsmen called Walloons were brought in from Belgium. The expense of the war brought Sweden's economy to the bottom. In a one-hundred-year period, the taxes were doubled and young men were forced into the military. These burdens hindered the farmers from tending to their farms. The cycle of hunger, disease, and unemployment was repeated.

The Swedish state had no money but plenty of land. In order to continue funding the war, the state sold much of that land, with thousands of acres coming under the ownership of the nobility. Toward the end of the seventeenth century, a few rich families controlled more than half of Sweden's farms. The upper nobility was at the height of its power and built several new and magnificent castles. The farmers were forced to leave their farms and take up residence on the less fertile lands at the outskirts of the nobility-owned estates. Common men had to work as many as five days a week for noblemen. The only way to improve their lot in life was to tend to the land surrounding their homes. But since that land, too, belonged to the noblemen, the more the farmers tried to improve their situation, the more work they ended up doing for the upper class. The Swedish farming class was on the verge of losing its freedom.

After the war, Sweden's territories were at their largest, ranging from Bremen and Pomerania to Skåne in today's southern Sweden, all of today's Finland and Estonia, and parts of Norway. Since more than one-fourth of Sweden's total population lived in the southern provinces, the territorial gains were substantive. It should be noted that control over Skåne, the most southern of the provinces, had been disputed many times. With the exception of the years 1332–60, Skåne had been part of Denmark. Control over the Baltic island of Gotland was also disputed several times, with Sweden gaining final control in 1645.

The Swedish Great Power reached its peak in 1658, and the country's participation in the Thirty Years' War opened up a long row of new possibilities. Sweden was affected by other European countries' cultural life and diversity, which allowed for the growth of Swedish art, poetry, and science. The clergy, the highest-educated members of society, did much of the administrative work. Through the mercenary system of using skilled foreigners with greater business sense than the

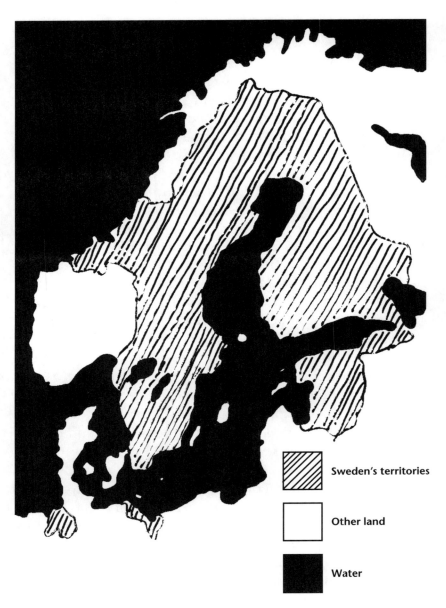

Sweden's territories

Other land

Water

Sweden's territories after the Thirty Years' War.

Swedes of the time, Gustav II Adolf's reign, together with Axel Oxenstierna, contributed to establishing an organized communication link with the rest of the world. Emphasis was placed on industry and commerce. New methods were developed for the mining of iron, laying the foundation for an industrialized Sweden.

The iron industry flourished, with the city of Bergslagen in middle Sweden at its center, as it still remains today. Walloons from Belgium and the Netherlands came to work at the foundries, and many of today's Swedish families are descendants of the Walloons. Trade benefited the state, foremost the capital of Stockholm, with centralized power finally making Stockholm the true capital of Sweden.

WOMEN'S ROLE

The seventeenth century is associated with war more so than any other time. Countless young men were called to serve in the military, and many never came back. This loss led to a surplus of young unmarried women. The lack of manpower forced women to handle duties at home that had previously been done by men. On the upside, this also gave women more independence. However, the seventeenth century also brought to the female population another problem: the witch-hunt.

The ancient belief in witches is found in almost every culture and was stromg in Europe in the Middle Ages. Due to the long lasting wars, many people feared that the destruction of the world was just around the corner. People intoxicated themselves with drink to get some relief from everyday life. The leaders, in turn, blamed the wars, hunger, and diseases on the devil and on the people's lack of a righteous living. It was decided that a prayer against the wrath of the devil be read at all worship services. A state commission was established to hunt down all who were thought to be allies of the devil. The church executed women accused of witchcraft, many of whom were pointed out by little children who did not know better. The crime often required a confession that could easily be drawn out through the use of torture, and hundreds of innocent women were beheaded or burned at the stake.

QUEEN KRISTINA AND HER SUCCESSORS

When Gustav II Adolf died in the Battle of Lützen, his daughter Kristina, who was his only heir, inherited the kingdom. Kristina was highly educated, could speak several languages, and participated in parliamentary meetings from the age of sixteen. She started to rule the kingdom in 1644 at the age of eighteen.

Kristina's higher education led to her longing to surround herself with people of equal standing. In contrast to her father, Kristina is said to have ruined Sweden's economy by spending a great deal of money on raising the current status of the nobility and exempting them from paying taxes. She invited nobles from Germany, England, Scotland, and France, and compensated them with land in return for bravery in battle. More than three hundred new families were added to the existing nobility. The power of the nobility grew larger by the day, until the land in more than half of Sweden was privately owned. In addition, much of the land owned by the nobility had previously been set aside to provision the military. This started an evil cycle. The more land the tax-exempt nobility owned, the less land was available for taxation. The military was weakened and in dire need of money to cover the expenses of the Thirty Years' War. The farmers were starving, and a failed harvest in 1649 placed beggars on every street corner. The relationship between the nobles and the commoners grew tense.

Long wars had driven the country's economy to rock bottom, and the farmers gathered at the parliament and expressed their complaints. The upper nobility was a threat to the rest of the people. The farmers demanded that the upper nobility return all of the land they had acquired from the state, so that the state could increase its income and reduce taxes. By now, even the clergy and lower nobility could feel the tax burden and joined in the farmers' demand for a reduction.

The farmers asked that Kristina protect them from the nobility. At the same time, the nobility asked that she protect them from the demands of the common man. It has been argued that Kristina might have had personal reasons for keeping the people divided, and that she took an opportune moment to use their discontent to her advantage: She suggested that her cousin, Karl Gustav, succeed her. In order to protect their estates against further reduction, the nobility agreed.

In 1654, Kristina abdicated and converted to Catholicism. People all over Europe were surprised. Kristina was the daughter of the Protestant king Gustav II Adolf, who had died in the Thirty Years' War and was considered, perhaps, the greatest spokesman for the rights of the Protestants. Kristina went to Rome and left the country in the hands of Karl X Gustav.

Karl X Gustav took an unexpected step when he, against Kristina's and the council's advice, forced the upper nobility to concede to a partial reduction of their land. Karl X Gustav's power among the common man was therefore strengthened. This success encouraged the people to use non-violence when making political decisions, and for the first time in more than a hundred years, a longer period of peace followed. The army was reorganized so that it could be supported by the state, and the new system of taxation meant a greater defense against tax increases for the farmers.

But the country was still threatened by its neighbors. The king set his focus on Poland first, from where he perceived the greatest threat, but he also faced attacks from Russian and Austrian armies. In 1657, Denmark declared war on Sweden. The Danish king Fredrik III set out with the hope of a weakened Swedish army, due to the conflict in Poland. But Karl X had no intention of staying in Poland and marched in on Denmark from the south. Since the Danish troops were in Sweden, much of Denmark was left undefended and the war was short lived, with Sweden easily defeating the remaining Danish soldiers.

Although Sweden was considered a great power with wide reaching territories, it lacked significant population and a forceful leadership. Prospective enemy countries surrounded its borders. The king needed an ally. He found one in Holstein-Gottorp, where he also found a bride, Hedvig Eleonora, who would bring him an heir to the throne. Karl XI was only four years old when his father died in 1660. Since he was too young to rule the country, another guardian government was established. When Karl XI finally took the throne in 1672, he carried through a major reform in military recruitment: the *indelningsverk*. The soldiers and officers were each given a cottage to live in and a piece of land to harvest. This gift was made possible through the prior reduction of land from the nobility, and was what enabled Sweden to keep a standing self-supporting army in peacetime. The more permanent living arrangements allowed the troops to meet at regular intervals for training. The officers resided in the area from which the soldiers were recruited, which eased problems of transportation and contributed to a feeling of pride in their regiments. This system was so attractive that it survived until 1901, when it was replaced by compulsory military service. The Karlskrona Naval Base was also founded during Karl XI's reign, with the intention of strengthening Sweden's presence in the Baltic Sea.

When Karl XI died in 1697, his fifteen-year-old son became king. Many regard Karl XII as Sweden's greatest war king. He is known for his many and long lasting travels throughout Europe, and for directing the first battles of the Great Nordic War.

Chapter Seven

Age of Freedom: 1700–1800

KARL XII

Karl XII became king of Sweden in 1697 at the age of fifteen, when his father Karl XI died. Since the new king was underage, a guardian government was established. However, the council was often at odds and lacked the power to act on important matters. It was therefore decided, approximately six months later, that the young Karl XII was mature enough and should come into full power as the ruling king of Sweden, despite the fact that he had not yet reached legal age.

Twenty years of peace had contributed to an upswing in the economy, and Karl XII attempted to continue the leadership that his father had started. He worked hard to eliminate the poverty that was a result of several years of bad crops. In addition, a fire at the Royal palace, Three Crowns, in Stockholm had recently annihilated the wooden castle, which needed to be rebuilt. These were peaceful ways in which the king attempted to improve the country. But he was also a man of strong will, a man driven to defend Sweden's power in the Baltic Sea, which was constantly threatened by the neighboring countries.

Initially, Karl XII sought to avoid the conflicts that plagued the rest of Europe, but he was interrupted by the outbreak of the Great Nordic War in 1700. Sweden was threatened from several directions, and without a strong army, it could not

The Royal Palace Tre Kronor (Three Crowns) was annihilated by fire in 1697. Model displayed at Stockholm City Museum.

defend all of its acquired land. Although Karl XII encouraged peace and strove to avoid military engagements, his political views failed to have lasting impact. And had the peace lasted, it might have isolated Sweden too much from the political interests of the rest of Europe.

The upper and lower nobility united to defend Sweden and sent the army out in yet another war. The rest of Karl XII's life was to be devoted to this war. Karl XII left Stockholm on a journey that would take him through several European nations, lasting until his death on a battlefield in Norway in 1718.

THE GREAT NORDIC WAR

The Great Nordic War was fought in northern and eastern Europe, 1700–21, and involved on the one side Sweden, and on the other a coalition between Sachsen-Poland, Denmark-Norway, and Russia.

In 1700, Sweden was a great power, which had, through its successful wars, become the dominating force in the area. Before Karl XI died in 1697, he had modernized the military, and the troops were highly trained and well equipped. The Swedish army was one of the best in Europe, and the young Karl XII inherited a well-oiled war machine. Since the dissolution of the Union of Kalmar, Sweden had aimed at controlling the Baltic Sea and the surrounding areas, with the result of repeated wars with Denmark and the other neighboring countries. In economic terms, the Baltic was Europe's most important body of water, which was a contributing factor in many wars fought in the region. Despite the fact that Sweden was sparsely populated and was mainly an agricultural society, the control over the Baltic provinces along with some territories in northern Germany gave Sweden great power, although it was a power position Sweden would be unable to maintain in the long run. Sweden was faced with many enemies, and the German territories were far away and spread apart, and required constant defense against foreign takeovers.

Sweden's prior enemies, Denmark, Poland, and Russia were convinced that the death of the old king had weakened Sweden and that the new king was too young and inexperienced to rule the country. Denmark had been a long-standing enemy of Sweden, and Denmark's King Fredrik IV wanted Skåne back and had his sights set on revenge. August the Strong of Poland strove to increase his power at home and turn the country into a threat to the rest of Europe. In addition,

135

Russia in the east was growing stronger and becoming a greater threat to Sweden in its desire to control the ports around the Baltic. Tsar Peter I wanted to increase Russia's power at sea. This objective required good harbors, which Russia, being more inland, lacked. A war with Sweden would give the tsar access to the Baltic-facing ports along Sweden's east coast. All these ambitions led Denmark, Poland, and Russia to join in an attempt to attack Sweden.

In 1697, the tension grew, and a conflict about the region Holstein-Gottorp resulted in war between Sweden and Denmark. To make matters worse, Denmark was trying to establish an alliance with Russia, through which it hoped to gain support for a hostile takeover of Sweden. Karl XII decided to go on the offensive against Denmark. However, Sweden's territories were not yet cohesive. Sweden had strong leadership but was weak otherwise and needed allies. Denmark-hating Holstein-Gottorp was the only ally Sweden could find at first.

In order that he might strengthen his standing against August of Poland and the Russian tsar Peter I, Karl XII had as a rule stayed neutral regarding the many European battles and stayed on good terms with the sea powers of England and Holland, who were more interested in trade than in controlling the seaports. Sweden entered into a treaty with England and Holland, which included the defense of Holstein-Gottorp against the Danes.

The king was initially successful at defending the Swedish territories, and in June 1700, Karl XII decided to fight Denmark first, then Poland. The Swedes closely observed the movements of the Danish army. With English and Dutch fleets assisting Sweden, the Danes were forced to retreat. After forcing Denmark back, Sweden was left with August of Poland, whose army was already at the border.

In 1700, the Polish king marched on Swedish soil. Karl XII felt that August of Poland was one of the least trustworthy of men, and that an attack on Poland was an absolute necessity if he were to avoid future threats. The Russians, on the other hand, were so far away and had such a long way to go that a surprise attack on Sweden seemed less credible. However, during the short time that Sweden was at war with Denmark, Russia took the opportunity to attack.

THE BATTLES OF NARVA AND POLTAVA

In November 1700, a Swedish army of eight thousand soldiers met a Russian army almost four times its size at Narva in modern day Estonia. But harsh weather and blowing snow made visibility exceptionally poor. As a result, the Russians assumed that the Swedes were retreating, when they were in fact pressing forward, and succeeded at taking the Russians by surprise. The Swedes attacked and split the much larger Russian army into three parts, which made victory easier. The Swedish losses were less than one-tenth of the Russian losses, and the Russians lost approximately ten thousand soldiers. The Battle of Narva was one of Sweden's biggest victories and a humiliating defeat for Russia. The victory made Karl XII famous throughout Europe. He was talked about as a true leader of men, unafraid and always at the front. The Russians were to make a grand comeback later after Tsar Peter had reorganized his army. But, for the time being, Karl XII had eliminated the immediate threat and could finally set his sights on August the Strong of Poland.

If Karl XII could dethrone August the Strong, he might be able to win Poland over and, thereby, win another ally in his struggle against Russia. But the war in Poland dragged on, and not until 1708 did Karl XII get the opportunity to again unite his army, now forty-four-thousand-man strong, against the great enemy in the east.

The winter of 1708–9 was bitterly cold. The soldiers suffered from frozen fingers and toes, and in some cases entire limbs had to be amputated. By spring, the Swedish army, which was now down to a meager half of its former strength, made camp near the Russian city of Poltava. Food for soldiers and horses was running out, and to make matters worse, Karl XII had been wounded in the foot and was forced to give up command to one of his generals.

At this point forty thousand rested Russian soldiers overpowered the Swedish army. The battle ended with almost seven thousand Swedish casualties, an additional three thousand taken prisoner, and fifteen hundred wounded. Karl XII managed to escape to Turkey, but half of Sweden's forces were eliminated in a single battle. This decimation was an unfathomable loss to Sweden's small population. The Battle of Poltava may be the greatest military catastrophe in Swedish history, and was a major factor in ending Sweden's role as a great power.

The Russians had taken many years to mount their comeback from the defeat at Narva, and now all land east of the Baltic was available to them. They pressed on into Finland. News of the loss also reached Denmark, which felt a need to re-enter the war. Now that the Swedes were weakened, a large Danish army could invade Skåne. It looked grim for Sweden, but epidemics and lack of food weakened the Danish advance, and in 1710, the Swedish army, led by a man named Magnus Stenbock, arrived in Skåne and defeated the Danish army. Russia, on the other hand, conquered the Baltic provinces, and forced Sweden to finally give up control of Finland. By 1715, Russia occupied Finland but was not overly concerned with keeping it. Rather, they wanted to use its bargaining power over Sweden. Denmark made a comeback and occupied Holstein-Gottorp, and again set its sights on Skåne.

THE INVASION OF NORWAY

In comparison to Sweden's few victories, the defeats were mounting up. Fourteen years of far-reaching wars both to the east and west had taken their toll, but the Swedish upper classes opposed a peace treaty with Denmark, because it would give bad trading privileges. The war dragged on, and once again the people suffered under high taxes, failed crops, disease, and forced recruiting of young men to the army. The farmers rebelled, and the officers didn't receive the same salaries as earlier. Houses and towns decayed because of lack of money and maintenance. Finally, only a small group of the king's closest men desired to continue the warfare.

Karl XII worked on strengthening the army, and in 1716 he attempted an attack on Kristiania (modern day Oslo) in Norway. Through the invasion, he strove to improve Swedish trade and increase bargaining power with Denmark, but his army was under-prepared and lacked sufficient artillery, and was forced to retreat. He also needed to guard Skåne, which was threatened by Tsar Peter and King Fredrik IV of Denmark. With a new army ready, Karl XII made another attempt on Norway. Sweden's enemies, who thought that Karl XII was ready for peace talks by now, were shocked when he instead moved forward to invade.

In his second attempt on Norway in 1718, Karl XII was better prepared, with enough soldiers, weapons, and food to supply an army of sixty thousand troops for six months. He left with the purpose of occupying Norway's most important agricultural sites and forts. But a wrench was about to be thrown into the wheel of these grand plans. In November 1718, the king was shot in the head and died on the spot. To this day it is not known whether the bullet came from the Norwegian side, was a stray from the Swedish side, or an intentional shot by one of the king's own people. Without leadership, the army was forced to retreat.

Although Karl XII's reign was heroic, it was not constructive. He had failed to retain the power of the monarchy and control of the Baltic, bringing Sweden's age as a great power to an abrupt end. Karl XII is a highly debated figure in Swedish history. On the one hand, he is seen as a national hero: courageous, faithful, and tolerant. On the other hand, he is criticized for being pigheaded and stubborn: a man who didn't use his diplomatic resources or listen to the advice of his council and generals. However, it is often the victors who write history, and had Karl XII not died on the battlefield, we might view him more favorably today.

In 1721, Sweden finally announced peace with its neighbors and lost almost all of its acquired territories around the Baltic Sea and the southeastern part of Finland. The loss of the territories and the peace treaty with Russia came as a severe blow to the Swedish population. Eighteen years of war had demoralized the people and taken a heavy toll on human life. Able young men were in the minority and many farms had to be run by women alone. Despite its losses, Sweden remained a powerful Nordic country. Although its territory was much smaller now, the country was also easier to defend in future conflicts. Ulrika Eleonora, Karl XII's sister, succeeded him to the throne on the condition that she would rule according to the advice of the parliament. The new constitution was drawn up with the intent to avoid absolute monarchy. But Ulrika Eleonora had little interest or education regarding politics, and later abdicated in benefit of her husband, Fredrik of Hessen, who was given the name Fredrik I.

THE AGE OF FREEDOM

The years 1718–72, following the Great Nordic War, are called the Age of Freedom and were a period of experimentation in

Photo taken in 1927 of a Swedish couple by the statue of Karl XII in Kungsträdgården (the king's garden) in Stockholm. Note how the king is pointing in the direction of the great enemy in the east: Russia. The mortars around the statue are war trophies from 1701.

semi-democratic processes, as opposed to absolute monarchy. France had a great influence on Sweden, particularly French designs in art and theater, such as operas, ballets, and masquerades. It was also a time of great achievement and development in science and literature. One of the most notable figures was Carl von Linne, a Swedish botanist and physician best known for his systematic classification of plants, animals, and minerals. Linne is by some considered the "Father of Botany." Also well-known are Anders Celsius, who developed the 100-degree thermometer that bears his name; Pehr Wilhelm, who developed a system of record keeping for births, deaths, and the movement of people (as a result, Sweden has the world's oldest official population statistics); and Carl Michael Bellman, a Swedish poet-musician who wrote parodies of life and the Bible.

The Swedish lifestyle changed with shifts in society that made everyone responsible for contributing to the economic welfare of the state. With the Freedom of the Press Act of 1766, political debates became more common. People were more inclined to express their opinions publicly, and to openly criticize the king and the government without fearing acts of reprisal. This atmosphere of open public expression helped lay a healthy foundation for a successful democracy.

The years between 1721 and 1740 were relatively peaceful, and over the rest of the century only a few short wars were fought. Lower taxes for the common man, good crops, population increase, and better trade helped the Swedish people back on their feet. The period was also relatively free of diseases, and a new crop, the potato, was introduced. The potato added nourishment, and was excellent for distilling *akvavit*, or *brännvin*, a high alcohol content liquor.

Taxes were kept low thanks to improved systems of taxation, and the farmers could keep their surplus. Development

During Carl Michael Bellman's life, 1740–95, Kungsträdgården (the king's garden) in Stockholm was a popular place for walks and outdoor activities, both among the nobility and the commoners.

of newer and better tools, including modern plows, led to improvements in farming. Better farming made it possible to divide the land and still live well. Many of those who had previously been forced to sell their farms could now re-buy their properties.

Sweden's exports consisted largely of iron, copper, and tar. In the less lucrative provinces, handicrafts, such as weaving and woodworking provided employment. The increased ability to specialize in particular kinds of work led to increased trade, which the state attempted to control. According to law, trading was allowed only in the cities. The buyers had a monopoly on the right to engage in trade, and the farmers had to pay a toll on their goods. However, this era also brought more control for the farmers through representation at the Riksdag (Parliament).

DEVELOPMENT OF THE PARLIAMENT

The people were generally disappointed with the power of the king, and the death of Karl XII brought an end to absolute monarchy. Fear of dominance by a single regent, and of foreign interference, and the overall poverty of the people motivated Sweden to build up its economy and encourage a parliamentary government. But this shift required strong leadership and the ability to survive while competing for position with the neighboring countries. The nobility felt they should have greater influence on Swedish society, and the rule of the kingdom now fell in the hands of the Riksdag.

The Riksdag included representatives from four Estates: the nobility, the clergy, the burghers, and the peasants, with the nobility being the largest group. In the new government, the dominant party appointed the council. The monarch was only one of several agencies with ruling power and had to rule

The Swedish parliament at the mouth of Old Town in the "city between the bridges." Note the tower of Storkyrkan in the background. The modern Riksdagshus was built between 1895 and 1904.

according to the will of the Estates and the advice of the Riksdag. In order for a proposal to become a law, it needed the consent of three of the four Estates. Therefore, the Riksdag had supreme power, with its council becoming Sweden's true regent. The monarchy was preserved, but only as a representative and not with any real ruling power.

The Riksdag met every third year and had the sole right to express the will of the people. In 1738, the Riksdag attained the power to vote against and unseat representatives who were not in agreement with the ruling parties. However, the uncontrolled power of the Riksdag led to damage when that power was abused. Since the Riksdag was controlled primarily by the upper classes with no outside checks, it had, in a sense, the same power as the king had had in earlier days.

The Riksdag elected committees. The Secret Committee handled anything of primary importance, such as questions regarding foreign policy and finance, or other matters that the nobility did not dare to entrust to the peasants. Although the farmers were not represented in the Secret Committee, they at least had a final say and influence regarding the decisions made at the Riksdag as a whole, which was a huge step forward for Sweden's peasant population.

Differences of opinion encouraged the formation of political parties. The first political parties were called Hattarna (the Hats) and Mössorna (the Caps). The Caps were given the nickname by the opposing party, the Hats, whose representatives were comprised mainly of the upper nobility. The Hats felt that the Caps were unsupportive of the Hats' desire to bring Sweden back as a great power. The Hats accused the Caps of weakness and exaggerated fear of war, acting like old ladies in nightcaps, unable to hold strong viewpoints about foreign policy. The Hats worked for the needs of the industry, favoring the aristocracy and a strong national defense, while the Caps worked for the needs of agriculture and Baltic trade, and favored peace.

Despite the war losses, the nobility wished to go back to the old days when they controlled most of the land. As soon as the state's economy had been strengthened, the nobility attempted to drag Sweden into yet another war in order to recapture some of its lost territories. But since the farmers had become stronger, they also had more say at the Riksdag and were able to preserve the peace for another twenty years, until 1741, when the nobility coerced the farmers' leadership into signing another declaration of war against Russia, in what became known as the "War of the Hats."

During the spring of 1743, Russian troops occupied the Baltic island of Åland on their way to Stockholm. Sweden's army was now forty-four thousand men strong, but was militarily unprepared and weak; it suffered considerable losses. The farmers were embittered and re-elected only one-fourth of their old representatives to the parliament.

The farmers feared that the Swedish capital would fall into the hands of the Russians. The farmers in one province, Dalarna, were particularly disgusted with the government and its lack of leadership in the war. They voiced their demands: lower taxes, free trade, a strong king to check the power of the nobility, and not only an end to the war but also the prosecution of those responsible. All who could use a rifle were encouraged to travel to Stockholm and help in the resistance. A mutinous peasant rebel-army, five thousand men strong, was formed to take part in Dalaupproret. Peasant armies from other provinces also got ready to march to Stockholm with guns and clubs, to demand that those responsible for the war be prosecuted and that the king's power be restored. The government fled in fear, but the farmers' hesitating leader held back the uprising. Stockholm's military called for stronger troops and prepared a counter-attack on the farmers. Several men from the peasant army were killed and their leader captured, after which a quick peace was instigated with Russia, with eleven thousand Russian soldiers hired to defend the Swedish nobility against further rebellions from the farmers or from Denmark, which again threatened war.

After Dalaupproret, the state lowered taxes and eased restrictions on trade. Although Sweden became Europe's leading exporter of iron, it still remained largely an agricultural society, with only a small percentage of the population living in the larger cities. Colonization of the lands in the north, which were inhabited by the Laps, a nomadic reindeer herding people, was encouraged and often led to conflicts. Still, the Age of Freedom had advanced the society, resulting in a surge of political debates and helping the people attain representation and freedom of expression.

THE GUSTAVIAN ERA

When Gustav III inherited the Swedish throne in 1771, his philosophy was that the power of the king should be increased. He also recommended that the tax burden should fall on only those who could afford to pay taxes. He therefore engaged in what turned out to be a bloodless battle with the state, ending the Age of Freedom. The nobility, who thought they were under-represented at the Riksdag with only one vote of four, initially supported the king in hope that he would increase their power, too. At the time, they didn't know that the king's goal was to level the nobles' power in order to increase his own. He established new laws that strained the relationship between king and nobility. The nobility felt threatened.

In the meantime, Gustav III continued searching for a way to control the Baltic Sea, but this goal would require another war with Russia. He strove for an alliance with Norway, but only if it excluded Denmark. A three-state alliance, such as the Union of Kalmar, was not possible. His war on Russia in 1788 was fought alone without the support of the other Nordic countries, and became nothing more than a series of small conflicts battled out along the Finnish border.

Gustav III admired France and French culture, and contributed much to cultural life. He was especially fond of the theater and opera. He had even written several plays, in which he himself played a part. But he was also disliked for his habit of instituting annoying laws, such as the prohibition of the right of citizens to privately distill *akvavit*. Initially, the law was introduced in an attempt to save the grain after a couple of years of crop failures and famine. Later, when the famine had passed, the king kept the state monopoly on *akvavit* for the sake of collecting revenue, and continued the prohibition. Needless to say, this law was unpopular with the peasants. It was constantly violated and did not achieve much success.

The power to institute new laws was divided between the king and the Riksdag. Still, in 1789, the king amended the law and restored absolute monarchy. The discontent among the people helped to build a powerful opposition party made up of nobles, and the price the king eventually had to pay was far higher than he had envisioned.

In a meeting at the Riksdag in 1792, the king and the nobles could not agree on how to regulate the state's debt. Eventually this impasse angered the nobles, who conspired to kill the king. The actual murder attempt took place in Stockholm in March 1792, at a dress ball at the Royal Opera, which Gustav III had founded. Despite several warnings about the planned assassination, Gustav III attended the ball. A bullet, fired by a man named Jacob Johan Anckarström, hit the king in the back. The king was fatally wounded, but didn't die from his injuries until approximately two weeks later. Anckarström was sentenced to death. His head and right hand were severed from his body and displayed on a pole for all to see. Anckarström became the last political criminal executed in Sweden.

Gustav III's underage son, Gustav IV Adolf, succeeded him to the throne, with his uncle acting as the guardian king. When Gustav IV came of age, he led much the same political life as his father had, which favored absolute rule of the monarchy. However, his lack of interest in domestic issues meant that the real power lay with the bureaucracy. In foreign affairs, he is best known for his opposition to the revolutionary France, which meant that Sweden lost its allies during the Napoleonic war.

Two treaties were signed early in the nineteenth century. In the treaty of Fredrikshamn, signed in 1809, Sweden ceded control of Finland, including the Åland Islands in the Baltic, to Russia. Many consider Gustav IV the primary person responsible for this loss, which included one-third of Sweden's territory and one-fourth of its population. But the loss of Finland meant more than just losing the territory that had acted as a buffer against Russia. The Swedish and Finnish people had grown accustomed to each other and embraced a similar culture. The Finnish people still have much in common with the Swedes and are seen as an integral part of Swedish history. In 1809, Sweden also signed a peace treaty with Denmark, without losing any more territory.

The new constitution of 1809 prescribed a division of power, where the king had to appoint a cabinet as his advisors and rule according to this council's advice. The king and Riksdag had veto power over each other, and approval of three of the four Estates was again needed in order to pass a new law. In 1810, a two-chamber Riksdag was recommended as a replacement for the outdated system of four Estates, but it was not to be realized for another fifty-five years.

Dissatisfaction with Gustav IV Adolf soon threatened a civil war. He was dethroned in a coup d'état in 1809, with his somewhat senile uncle, Karl XIII, succeeding him.

Chapter Eight
Age of Liberalism: 1800–1900

JEAN-BAPTISTE BERNADOTTE

In the beginning of the nineteenth century, Sweden went outside of the country's borders to look for strong leadership and a suitable successor to the throne, which it found in a French marshal named Jean-Baptiste Bernadotte. Karl XIII, who lacked children of his own, adopted the forty-seven-year old Frenchman and gave him the Swedish name Karl XIV Johan. Jean-Baptiste didn't become king until 1818 when Karl XIII died, but he was in effect the ruling king from 1810.

Jean-Baptiste had joined the French army in 1780, at the age of seventeen, where he made quick progress and achieved the rank of general in 1794. Later, as one of Napoleon's most skilled leaders, he became marshal of France. But he was to get into numerous disagreements with Napoleon, something Sweden couldn't have known when it offered Jean-Baptiste the title of crown prince.

When Napoleon agreed to let Jean-Baptiste leave France for Sweden, he asked the marshal that, if fate would have it, he would not enter into war against France. Jean-Baptiste answered that he would make no such promise, stressing that he could only accept the position of crown prince of Sweden if he could also place Sweden's well-being and interests at the forefront. Napoleon is then said to have answered: "Go then, and let our destinies be fulfilled." Later, Sweden joined the British-led alliance against Napoleon.

The choice of Jean-Baptiste as crown prince of Sweden was made in the hope that he would establish an alliance with France and, with France's help, re-acquire Finland from Russia. However, the selection of the French general didn't result in the expected cooperation between France and Sweden against Russia. Jean-Baptiste's policies were predominantly peaceful, and much progress was made in commerce and culture instead.

The Age of Liberalism was characterized by society's struggle toward economical and political freedom, such as freedom of speech, press, and religion, and against giving certain groups of people privileges over others. In contrast to the many previous changes the Swedish people had gone through, the introduction of liberalism took place under peaceful circumstances. Jean-Baptiste succeeded in leading Sweden on the road toward industrialization, and his strong leadership helped re-establish the people's belief in the future.

UNION WITH NORWAY

One of Karl XIV Johan's (Jean-Baptiste Bernadotte) most important political decisions was to form an alliance with Russia rather than with France, in the hope that Russia would help Sweden acquire Norway from Denmark. Sweden would, in exchange for Russia's help, fight against Napoleon's army in Pomerania and Leipzig. The king's desire for Norway was more strategic than economic; he thought it would give the Swedish people a feeling of prestige after their loss of Finland. The union with Norway led to expectations of strength and safety, and Karl XIV felt that expanding Sweden's territories by moving west instead of east would strengthen the country's bond with Russia.

The battle in Leipzig lasted only three days before Sweden and Russia achieved victory. Sweden then marched against Denmark, resulting in Denmark's quick defeat and the Treaty of Kiel, which stipulated the conditions on which Sweden was to acquire Norway. The Treaty of Kiel, signed by the Danish king Fredrik VI in 1814, stated that Norway should come under full possession of Sweden. In return, Swedish Pomerania was given to Prussia. This exchange also eased Sweden's control of its territories, now that it had only one contiguous landmass to worry about.

But the Norwegians were unable to find an attraction in Swedish land and people, and had little desire to unite with the Swedes. Sweden had been engaged in almost constant warfare and was viewed as an aggressive country, and after having been in union with Denmark for several hundred years, Norway wished to be independent. In addition, the Norwegians couldn't find any economic advantage in a union with Sweden, as the land and resources in Sweden and Norway were so similar that they overlapped rather than complemented one another. This disinclination resulted in Karl XIV having to invade Norway and force the Norwegians to submit to the union. That brief war with Norway in 1814 is the last war in which Sweden has been involved. Overall, Karl XIV Johan encouraged neutrality and, since he became king in 1818, avoided involvement in other countries' interests. Later, during the Crimean War between Russia and Turkey in 1853, Sweden considered joining the battle alongside of Russia, but the thought of yet another war resulted in restraint and a declaration of neutrality. After such a turbulent past, the Swedish people longed to be left alone, left only to defend their nation if need be, and not to enter into wars or alliances with others.

The union between Sweden and Norway lasted until 1905, when it was dissolved peacefully. It was decided that maintaining a union between two countries with force made the price greater than the value. When the union had been dissolved, the Swedish government was finally free to place full emphasis on the condition of Sweden. Feelings of resentment eased, and in the years to come more doors would open for a cooperative and friendly relationship with Norway.

INDUSTRIAL DEVELOPMENT

In 1807, Sweden underwent a grand agricultural reform. Villages were split, allowing farmers to live closer to their land. The country also saw a large population increase. Although its birthrate remained largely the same, long lasting peace, better food, and vaccines against and education about diseases helped people live longer. In the first fifty years of the nineteenth century, Sweden's small population of 2.3 million increased to 3.5 million. Most Swedes lived in rural areas, with the population of the cities accounting for a mere 10 percent. But better technology helped catapult industrialization forward, leading to the building of factories and mass production of goods. Exports of iron and timber increased, and the building of railroads in the 1850s required much manpower, made transport of goods easier, and helped end rural isolation. In the later part of the nineteenth century and the beginning of the twentieth century, Sweden's population almost doubled from 3.5 million to 6 million people.

This increase created certain problems. A strong middle-class emerged, which strove to increase its standard of living and fought against the upper classes. At the beginning of the nineteenth century, two new classes were established: the working class, which owned neither land nor tools and earned its living by working for others, and the business class, which earned its living based on agriculture and trade. Now, with a surplus of money, the business class could invest in other businesses, industries, and modern farm equipment, and could hire lower class people to work with these new tools and machines.

The nineteenth century brought the establishment of several new industries. One of the era's famous industrialists was L.M. Ericsson (Lars Magnus Ericsson), who started as a toolmaker in 1870, and whose telephone manufacturing company later transformed the industry with its focus on the development of mobile telephones (cell phones) and other wireless technology. The L.M. Ericsson company was founded in 1876 and has, into the modern day, remained Sweden's pride. Developments were also made in ball bearings, with Svenska Kullagerfabriken (Swedish Ball Bearing Factory) founded in 1907, and in matches and explosives, such as the Swedish safety match and Alfred Nobel's nitroglycerin, or dynamite. The revenues from Alfred Nobel's factories led to the establishment of the prestigious Nobel Prize in science, literature, and peace. Alfred Nobel specified in his will that his fortune be awarded each year "to those who, during the preceding year, shall have conferred the greatest benefit on mankind."

The furniture and handicraft industry also grew. One craft of standing value is the Dalahäst or Dala horse, from Dalarna, north of Stockholm. The horse was a good friend to the family and a highly valued farm animal that became a symbol of strength and loyalty. Since the 1840s, horses of varying sizes have been carved from single pieces of wood and painted red with colorful patterns. These horses are then sold as toys or for decoration, a tradition that remains into modern day.

Two Dalahästar: *one in the shape of a full horse seven inches tall and the other a smaller head to be hung on the wall.*

With the transition toward an industrial society, more women started to work outside of the home. In 1842, public education was made compulsory, elementary schools were introduced, and with the help of the Lutheran Church, illiteracy became almost extinct among the younger generation. But it still took many years before the educational system was universally established.

Literature became an important part of Swedish culture. Some of the most influential authors to come out of this were August Strindberg, Selma Lagerlöf (who received the Nobel Prize in literature in 1909), and Astrid Lindgren (who wrote *Pippi Långstrump*, translated as *Pippi Longstocking*, and many other cherished works for children).

The nobility attempted to establish new laws to interfere with industrial development; for example, laws that prohibited people from moving and working wherever they chose, or laws that prohibited the business class from establishing industries, if it was determined that doing so would harm the nobility. With the advent of capitalism, those who were financially strong could exercise power over those with less. In short, the ability to earn and accumulate money determined a person's power. For example, the worker received a salary, often too small and barely enough to enable him to survive. Rather than paying out larger salaries, much of the profit of the business class was invested in other businesses, increasing production with even greater profits. But this increase created a new problem: With modern machines came the ability to manufacture a surplus. In conjunction with low salaries among the working class, nobody could afford to buy the goods manufactured. Unemployment followed. The workers earned even lower salaries or were terminated from their jobs. These sorts of economic crises were common in the nineteenth century and often went in cycles.

As one of the poorer nations in Europe, Sweden moved into industrialism decades behind its Western counterparts. But within another hundred years, Sweden would move away from agriculture and become one of the most industrialized and prosperous countries in the world. A combination of governmental, economic, and individual forces in science, technology, and politics, along with a longer period of peace, left Sweden free to focus on welfare and the modernization of society.

FOLK MOVEMENTS

The Swedish democratic tradition started its development in the working class. The old ruling class, the nobility, was beginning to see its own end. The common man felt that it was unreasonable that the nobles should have certain privileges only because they were born into noble families. In the Riksdag, the working class and the business class fought for a free society, where people could work wherever they pleased. Democratic movements grew among the craftsmen, farmers, workers, and businessmen, who argued that all people should have equal value, and that society should be based on freedom and equality. Radical newspapers emerged, which criticized the nobility and supported the democratic movements. Many of these papers were censored and the editors imprisoned, but the government was unable to quiet the opposition.

In 1830, *Aftonbladet* (*The Evening Post*), a daily newspaper that is still in print today, was founded. *Aftonbladet* has a long and interesting history, including numerous conflicts with the authorities. The king had the right to retract the permission to publish the newspaper, and whenever *Aftonbladet* criticized him, he shut it down. The paper would immediately start up again under a slightly different name: The Second

Modern copy of Aftonbladet, *Sweden's oldest, biggest, and most influential daily newspaper.*

Aftonbladet, The Third *Aftonbladet,* The Fourth *Aftonbladet,* and so on. The king finally tired around the publication of The Twenty-Eighth *Aftonbladet.* The civil service officer responsible for revoking the newspaper's license declared the method useless and allowed the newspaper to remain in print. *Aftonbladet* developed into the most influential and widely read daily newspaper in the country.

During the nineteenth century, several folk movements grew and became strong democratic forces. These factions included temperance movements against the drinking of spirits, and free churches that wanted to interpret the Bible themselves and refuse state control. Both of those were democratic organizations, where every member, man and woman, had the right to vote. Public parades were organized to express the will of the people. The folk movements also gave the less educated classes an opportunity to learn how to express themselves and practice their critical thinking skills regarding social issues. This exercise led to a greater understanding of politics, and the feeling that the common man was not powerless. Women's movements also developed, but most noteworthy for the time may have been the labor movements.

A large part of the population belonged to the working class. However, this class lacked what is today considered every Swedish citizen's right: a regulated workweek, fair pay, pensions, and vacation and sick leave benefits. Unemployment contributed to the need to unionize and fight for higher salaries, healthier working conditions, prohibition of labor on Sundays and holidays, and an eight-hour workday. The strike was the workers' greatest weapon. But in order for a strike to be successful, the workers needed to unite, with large numbers participating. *Fackföreningar* (labor unions) were formed that strove toward better relations between employers and workers. In 1909, perhaps the greatest strike in Sweden's history took place. It exempted only public health and safety workers. The strike, like most strikes of this time period, failed to accomplish its objective of better wages. Not until ten years later did the labor union finally succeed at regulating the eight-hour workday. From then on, social democrats would dominate politics in most Swedish towns.

The threat to employers was growing now that they knew that the workers had the capacity to organize a sizable strike. Strikes sometimes required the military to step in and keep the workers under control. In 1931, five workers were shot to death during a military intervention. The employers tried to force new laws against the unions, or split the workers by encouraging them to cross the picket line. But the unions kept growing in size and power. The LO Landsorganisationen (Confederation of Trade Unions) has today more than 2 million members, a significant number considering the fact that Sweden's total workforce numbers only 4.5 million. In 1938, an agreement between the workers' unions and the employers resulted in a change in relations, with future strikes and conflicts becoming short-lived.

In a congress in Paris 1889, it was decided that May 1 should be an international holiday, symbolizing the continued struggle for the rights of the workers. In Sweden on this day, the workers and politicians march, demonstrate, and speak on issues concerning labor and well-being.

DEVELOPMENT OF POLITICAL PARTIES

In the eighteenth century, the Hats and the Caps had emerged at the Riksdag. But Sweden did not really have any true political parties until 1889, when the Social Democratic Worker's Party, which helped organize the unions, was formed. The head of the first social democratic government in Sweden was

Hjalmar Branting, who had distinguished himself through his diplomacy and work on a peaceful solution to the Swedish-Norwegian union. He became the first social democrat elected to the second chamber in the Riksdag in 1896, and in 1921 was awarded the Nobel Peace Prize.

Around the turn of the twentieth century, the Conservative, Liberal, and Social Democratic party groupings emerged. Today, seven parties are represented at the Riksdag, from largest to smallest in the 2002 election: Socialdemokratiska Arbetarpartiet (the Social Democratic Worker's Party, 39.8 percent of the vote), Moderata Samlingspartiet (the Moderates, or the Right Wing Party, 15.5 percent of the vote), Folkpartiet (the Liberal Party, 13.3 percent of the vote), Kristdemokraterna (the Christian Democratic Party, 9.1 percent of the vote), Vänsterpartiet (the Left Party, formerly the Communists, 8.3 percent of the vote), Centerpartiet (the Center Party, with agrarian dominance, 6.1 percent of the vote), and Miljöpartiet (the Green Party, with focus on the environment, 4.6 percent of the vote). Only parties that obtain at least 4 percent of the votes are represented at the Riksdag. Sweden's political parties are aligned into two blocks, the rights (conservatives), and the lefts (socialists). Despite the many elections that have taken place, Sweden has remained largely a social democratic country. Except for a few months in 1936, the social democrats remained in constant power from 1932 until 1976, when the right-wing coalition took over until 1982.

ON THE ROAD TO DEMOCRACY

The new constitution of 1809 had principles of lasting value. Legislative power was divided between the king and the Riksdag, and the king had to take the advice of his council.

Sweden has since then become one of the most stable democracies in the world. However, the government consisted for a long time of a select minority of men. In the old Riksdag, the nobility still held much of the power and supported the monarchy. The nobility also had a greater chance of holding higher offices than the common man.

In 1866, the Riksdag was reformed into a two-chamber (bicameral) system, which meant an end to the outdated system of four Estates. The two chambers of the new Riksdag represented the upper classes and the commoners. The establishment of the bicameral system had its greatest positive impact on farmers. With the introduction of the bicameral system, the clergy was no longer represented, yet the church continued serving the state by keeping records of births, deaths, and movement of people. Despite these improvements, the new Riksdag of the mid-1800s was not yet democratic—it still grossly favored the male population and the business class. For example, the right to vote was granted only to men, and only to those earning a substantial income, which accounted for about 6 percent of the population.

Voting rights had been a major political question since the end of the nineteenth century, and the one issue that precluded Sweden from becoming a true democracy. In 1902, one hundred and twenty thousand workers went on strike for three days to fight for their right to vote. Women lacked the right to vote. When people started giving this issue serious thought, many considered excluding women a waste of half of the nation's resources. Were women really so different from men that it warranted withholding education and voting rights? Changes are often known to take hundreds of years, but the issue of women suffrage had been ripening for some time, and it was also noted that no great catastrophe had happened in the neighboring Nordic countries, where women had already gained the right to vote.

The newspaper *RÖSTRÄTT FÖR KVINNOR* (*Right to Vote for Women*) questioned whether women truly were unable to cast an intellectual vote, and stated in the June 1, 1912, issue:

Motto: Vi kunna aldrig göra så mycket för en stor sak som en stor sak kan göra för oss. (Motto: We can never do as much for a grand cause as a grand cause can do for us.)

Kvinnorna har funnit vägen till fabriker, kontor, skolor, läkarbefattningar, överallt i samhällsarbetet deltaga de. Kan det då vara rättvist att säga, att de icke få deltaga i avgörandet av fosterlandets angelägenheter? Kan det vara möjligt, att de skola vara dugliga och skickliga i sitt yrke, men att en oöverstiglig mur skiljer dem från fosterlandets angelägenheter? (Women have found their way to factories, offices, schools, the medical profession, they participate everywhere in society. Can it then be fair to say that they should be banned from participating in decisions regarding the nation's interests? Can it be true that they are capable and skilled in their occupations, but that an insurmountable wall separates them from our nation's interests?)

> —Karl Staaff, Swedish liberal prime minister who fought for justice and the universal right to vote.

Not until 1909 was the right to vote granted to all men and, not until ten years later, to all women. After the 1921 election, five women were chosen to the parliament. Therefore, Sweden became a true democracy in 1921.

The bicameral parliament survived until 1971, when it was replaced by a unicameral system. Today, the Swedish

Riksdag has, in comparison to parliaments of other nations, a large number of female representatives. In fact, with nearly half of the seats occupied by women, Sweden has a larger percentage of female representation than any other country. But it was not until recent years that women acquired this kind of equality. Not until around 1950 did the female representation reach 5 percent in the first chamber and 10 percent in the second chamber. In 1970, women accounted for only 13 percent of the total representation at the *Riksdag*. The number increased to 38 percent by 1988, and 43 percent by 1994. The last thirty years saw the most significant breakthrough. One reason for this increase might be a number of strong women's rights organizations, another a conscious effort by the Swedish political parties to include an equal number of female representatives.

In 1975 the king lost his last political influence, and today Sweden finally has a true parliamentary government, where the people elect the Riksdag and the government must govern according to the will of the Riksdag or consider resigning. The king acts as a ceremonial head of state, but without any ruling power.

EMIGRATION TO AMERICA

Despite its rapid development, Sweden was still mostly a poor agricultural country. Overseas trade was hit hard during the first part of the nineteenth century, mostly by the Napoleonic wars, creating stagnation in the economy. In addition, a longer time of peace, successful vaccinations against diseases, and the discovery of the nutritious potato caused people to live longer, and Sweden's population doubled. This led to a lack of land, which resulted in unemployment. The only thing the farmers owned was their ability to work, and many families had to leave their farms and seek employment elsewhere. Children were forced into the working life to help provide for themselves and their relatives. Many families saw no future in Sweden and, in search of a better life, emigrated across the Atlantic Ocean to America, sometimes never to be heard from again.

Emigration started in earnest in the mid-1840s, with mass emigration reaching its peak during the economic crises between 1866 and 1914. During these years, almost one-fifth of Sweden's population left. The great crop failure, which was the result of an overly wet year in 1867 then an overly dry one in 1868, led to epidemics and a famine, and transportation of food to the affected areas was difficult. Farmers made up almost 80 percent of the population, and large families were forced to divide their land into tiny holdings that were fragmented and difficult to cultivate. The farmers were the largest group affected.

Most of those who left did so because of their discontent with the economic situation and with class differences. They were drawn to America by the Homestead Act of 1862, which granted 160 acres of free land to anyone who would live on it and work it for five years. Some of the younger generation fled the compulsory military service or simply gave in to their longing for adventure. Many Swedes also left because they were not yet so impoverished that they had stopped dreaming, and they lived in a relatively free society that kept the lines of communication open. Advertisements and letters from relatives who had already emigrated served to convince others to follow. But the letters were often misleading, speaking of a better life in America than what reality had to offer.

The Swedish people went mainly to New York, and then on to Iowa, Illinois, and Minnesota where the climate was familiar. Most Swedes adapted well and were able to contribute to the development of their new nation, despite the many more hardships that met them once they arrived in America. Still, most also continued speaking their native language, upheld their traditions, and would often longingly look back and refer to Sweden as "det gamla landet" (the old country).

Vilhelm Moberg, one of Sweden's foremost twentieth century writers, gives an excellent account of the emigration movement through his classic four-volume series on peasants from southern Sweden who leave to build a new life in Minnesota: *Utvandrarna* (*The Emigrants*), *Invandrarna* (*Unto a Good Land*), *Nybyggarna* (*The Settlers*), and *Sista Brevet till Sverige* (*The Last Letter Home*). His works are genuinely Swedish and speak of the dreams, desires, fears, and everyday struggles of the people of this era.

By 1910, 1.4 million first and second generation Swedes lived in the United States. This number was significant compared to Sweden's total population of 5.5 million people. But the Swedish people were not the only emigrants. Emigration affected other northern European countries as well, with Ireland and Norway surpassing Sweden in the number of emigrants in proportion to their population. The country's new railroad system, along with organized traffic across the Atlantic, often on British or German ships, made these large movements possible. The first few trips by sailboat took more than two months to complete. As the ships were upgraded to steam, the travel time was cut to three weeks in the best cases. People's diaries give us a good idea of what it was like, with seasickness, rancid food, and over-crowding. The voyage was often so rough that, despite their longing for home, the emigrants dreaded the return trip so much that it never materialized. Between 10 and 20 percent of the emigrants eventually returned to Sweden. On the positive side, the great movement of people promoted the exchange of ideas across nations and enabled both Sweden and the United States to progress. Later, with the coming of World War I and the Great Depression, emigration was brought to a halt.

Despite this mass emigration, Sweden has also, from Ice Age to present day, been a country of immigrants, with many cultures represented within its borders. Especially between 1930 and 1970, the economy was to be on the upswing and Sweden was to become an immigrant country, with industries recruiting skilled workers from Finland, Yugoslavia, and Mediterranean countries such as Italy, Greece, and Turkey, to fill job vacancies. In 1972, Sweden stopped its recruitment of non-Nordic labor.

BRIEF HISTORY OF ALCOHOL CONSUMPTION

The Swedes are generally known for being heavy social drinkers as well as binge drinkers. Their affinity for alcoholic beverages dates back to at least the Viking Age. Some have attributed Sweden's alcohol problem to the long and cold winters when people drank to stay warm, or spent most of their time indoors and drank because there wasn't much else to do. However, a more reasonable explanation might lie in the discovery of the potato. As early as 1467, *akvavit* (hard liquor) was imported from Lübeck to be used, primarily, as an ingredient in the production of gunpowder. In 1494, Sten Sture the Elder predicted that drinking would become a problem for the Swedish people and issued a law forbidding distilling or sale of *akvavit* in Stockholm. In 1746, it was discovered that the potato was excellent for distilling. The potato was grown in abundance and was readily available even among the poorer farming population.

In the nineteenth century, the average Swede was consuming forty-six liters of alcohol per year. Such excess inspired the temperance movement against drinking. King Karl XIV Johan (Jean-Baptiste Bernadotte) proclaimed that alcohol would be the ruin of the Swedish people. He requested that all churches in the country educate their congregations about temperance societies. Employers also supported the temperance movement because hangovers made most workers practically useless on Mondays. In 1855, the government passed a law forbidding the distilling of alcohol at home.

In 1905, the state took control of all sales of strong liquor. In 1955, Systembolaget, the state-owned Swedish network of liquor stores, gained a monopoly on selling wine and hard liquor and took responsibility for controlling the population's drinking habits. Sweden has one of the toughest anti-alcohol policies in Europe—alcohol is heavily taxed, with the tax accounting for approximately 70 percent of the price. If you add to this the regular sales tax, you might pay up to 80 percent in tax, for example, on a bottle of Absolut Vodka. (Sweden is considering changing the tax law. The other Nordic nations have already lowered their alcohol tax in an attempt to keep their population from traveling to buy large amounts of alcohol from more favorably taxed countries).

In many ways, the population seemed to favor restricted drinking habits. A poll in 1910 indicated that a slight majority favored permanent prohibition, but that wasn't an official vote organized by the government, and a new law against drinking was never instituted. A direct vote in 1922 resulted in a slight margin of 51 percent against and 49 percent for total prohibition. So, the result was a continuation of the rationing system.

In 1917, Sweden had begun rationing alcohol through the use of the liquor ration book, the *motbok*. The idea was to control drinking habits, so that nobody could buy more than what one could safely drink without harming oneself or others. Men were allowed to buy more than women. The *motbok* was abolished in 1955 and replaced with the *spärrlista*. Only those who had had a brush with the law because of their drinking habits were placed on this list and banned from buying more alcohol. In 1977, the *spärrlista* was abolished, but Systembolaget's monopoly on sale of alcohol remained. In 1982, Systembolaget decided to close its stores on Saturdays (the stores were already closed on Sundays). In 2001, Systembolaget reopened on Saturdays.

The state-owned Systembolaget frequently advertises against its own products: *När hade du sist en vit vecka?* (When was the last time you had a white week? [a week without any alcohol consumption]). Systembolaget strives to educate people on how to drink in moderation for joy and tradition, without harming themselves or others.

The legal drinking age in Sweden is twenty. Most people refrain from drinking during the week, but when Friday afternoon comes, the lines outside the liquor store can stretch a quarter of a mile long. Some of those buyers then spend most of the weekend drinking. This is not true for the entire population, and in fact, only 3–4 percent of Sweden is considered alcoholic. Statistics show that Sweden ranks around twentieth place for alcohol consumption among the industrialized nations of the world.

Although most Swedes drink only occasionally, when they do, it is often with the goal of getting drunk. If we consider the consumption of alcohol over time, the average Swede today drinks less than the equivalent average citizen of 150 years ago would have. The average consumption of forty-six liters of *brännvin* (hard liquor) per person per year in 1829 amounts to about ten times the modern average consumption. In later years, there has also been a decrease in hard liquor drinking and an increase in wine and beer. While the consumption of hard liquor has been cut in half since 1955, the consumption of wine and beer has increased twenty-fold!

Since Sweden received full membership in the European Union in 1995, the country does not have supreme authority to make decisions regarding the import and export of alcohol. The European Union has decided that Sweden is allowed to keep Systembolaget for now. However, the monopoly on import, export, and the sale of liquor to restaurants was banned. Due to pressure from the European Union to lower trade barriers, the alcohol import laws were relaxed in the beginning of 2004. The idea of monopoly is generally not looked favorably upon by the consumer, anyway. The people of Sweden argue that they should have the right to decide if, when, and how much they want to drink. Since the state's monopoly on alcohol distribution has been threatened, Swedish society has undergone considerable changes aimed at popularizing Systembolaget among the people. Whether the network will survive remains to be seen.

Chapter Nine

First and Second World Wars: 1900–1950

WORLD WAR I

Sweden's most aggressive period was in the 1600s, when the country was engaged in warfare for more than two-thirds of the century. In the 1700s, the war years were cut in half, and in the 1800s, the war years were cut to fewer than five. The last war Sweden fought was in 1814, which resulted in the acquisition of Norway. Since then, Sweden has upheld a strong policy of neutrality and has escaped warfare. Some critics consider this evasion to be mostly the result of luck, or worse, questionable ethics.

The First and Second World Wars had, despite Sweden's non-participation, lasting impact, particularly regarding the export and import of necessary goods such as food and energy. In 1912, the tension in Europe was so great that Sweden expected the outbreak of a world war and began planning for how to meet the difficulties that lay ahead, while at the same time upholding the country's wishes to remain neutral. The war preparations included hurried attempts to establish new laws banning the export of weapons and other war-related material. Laws were also instituted regarding the rationing of fuel and food, such as meat, eggs, bread, butter, and coffee, which seriously affected the heavy coffee-drinking Swedes. Sugar was rationed to no more than one kilo per person per month.

The king, Gustav V, took an active approach regarding the nation's defense. For example, he approved a demonstration, and criticized the Prime Minister for wanting to cut back on the military. In 1914, *bondetåget* (the farmer's march) of thirty-one thousand expressed their support for the king and the defense program, and offered to contribute to the army and fleet with their knowledge and abilities. The king publicly addressed the participants of the demonstration, discussed the possibility of Sweden joining the war, and expressed support for Germany. Since the cabinet council had not given their consent to the king's public speech, the cabinet resigned, and the king had to appoint a new cabinet without the support of the parliament.

Shortly after the start of the war, Sweden proclaimed complete neutrality and took defensive measures, such as placing ships along its coastline to protect its neutrality and prevent territorial violations. Although an agreement to a defensive alliance was obtained with Norway, many of the politicians felt that such an alliance with any country would not work to Sweden's advantage, because it might ultimately tempt the Swedish people to get involved in potential conflicts that Norway might have with other countries. As a whole, the Swedish people were firmly determined to stay neutral. Those who disagreed regarding this matter tended toward a pro-German attitude. Some felt that an alliance with Germany, against Russia, might help Sweden to check further Russian expansion, to turn Finland into a buffer zone between Sweden and Russia, and to gain the possibility of annexing the Åland Islands. The Åland Islands, located approximately halfway between Sweden and Finland, were a strategic concern. Also, this program appealed to many Swedes who still regretted the loss of Finland. Since the Åland Islands were inhabited mostly by a Swedish-speaking population, Sweden felt that the islands should rightfully belong to Sweden.

The leading social democrats were generally pacifists and had a strong interest in peace. Sweden informed Germany of its wishes to remain neutral, but agreed to exercise a "Germany friendly" neutrality. This general attitude lasted until 1917, when new views on the war led to a parliamentary shift toward a more British friendly attitude. Germany criticized Sweden's neutrality declaration and accused the Swedish king of taking first prize in spinelessness.

Despite careful preparations, Sweden's territories were violated several times. For example, German ships sunk two Swedish vessels carrying a cargo of timber. The Swedish government protested heavily and requested compensation. The British placed mines in trade routes in order to prevent Swedish trade with Germany. In May 1918, a large minefield was discovered within Swedish territory, which resulted in the destruction of three Swedish fishing ships and the deaths of fourteen fishermen.

Although Sweden was a great exporter of goods to Germany, the Swedish people's standard of living worsened during the war, and demonstrations and strikes took place all over the country. Even the military conscripts' solidarity was questioned. But the real problem was feeding the people. Despite rationing, food was difficult to come by in poorer communities. The lack of imported goods and a poor harvest in 1917 affected the availability of both meat and produce, and drove up prices. The closing of trade routes was also a contributing factor. Both Britain and Germany banned the export of coal for fuel to Sweden, unless Sweden also exported iron, steel, and other products to these countries. Matters were made worse when England and the United States required the use of Swedish ships for their own transports, in order to allow exports of the most important goods to Sweden. Still, it was difficult for Britain to completely shut off the Swedish trade of iron ore with Germany.

ACTIVE NEUTRALITY

Finland's declaration of independence from Russia in 1917 resulted in a political power struggle in Finland, which led to a full civil war. Since Sweden had declared neutrality, it could not openly display any participation in the war. However, Sweden organized a voluntary force, The Swedish Brigade, of more than a thousand men who attempted to mediate in the civil war in Finland. One of the first to volunteer his services was Olof Palme, uncle of Sweden's future prime minister, Olof Palme. The elder Palme was one of the Swedes killed in the conflict.

Sweden's goal in volunteering its help was two-fold: to make Finland a part of Sweden again and to come to the aid of its former Finnish brothers. Sweden also had a strategic interest in the Åland Islands for the defense of Stockholm. However, to Sweden's disappointment, the Finns, just like the Norwegians, desired to be independent. The question of whether the Åland Islands should be Swedish or Finnish would continue to be disputed for some time. The Åland Islands are culturally as Swedish as the islands of Gotland and Öland; however, although the Åland Islands have achieved autonomy, they remain to this day a part of Finland.

A recurrent question was to what extent Sweden should exercise its neutrality. Restraint was necessary in order to assume a strictly defensive role, but the Swedes often felt that they should help the other Nordic countries with voluntary manpower. Sweden also desired to concern itself with fundamental human rights, and participated in many humanitarian and peacekeeping operations throughout both world wars. Sweden became a member of the United Nations in 1946 and has since then made an active commitment regarding foreign policy, including participation in most peacekeeping operations. Through its membership in the United Nations, Sweden devotes a percentage of its national income to the developing countries.

After World War I, Sweden took on "active neutrality." The country could now exercise economic sanctions, but not participate with military forces. Later, in World War II, Sweden shipped necessities such as food, medical supplies, and pre-fabricated houses to Norway.

In the Finnish Winter War of 1939, after Germany's quick attack and victory over Poland, the defenders of Finland fought against attacks from Russia. Sweden had previously agreed with Finland to occupy the Åland Islands if Finland was threatened by war and to help Finland against the Russian invasion. However, although there were strong pro-Finland feelings among the Swedish people, Sweden desired to remain a non-participant in the war and instead sent Finland material and humanitarian help, including weapons and almost ten thousand Swedish volunteers.

Sweden also accepted thousands of refugees and partici-pated in a massive operation to evacuate around seventy thou-sand Finnish children to Swedish foster care. During World War II, Sweden received more than a million refugees and other immigrants. Sweden also arranged for the release of nearly twenty thousand prisoners from German concentration camps, to be transported to Swedish hospitals. Count Folke Bernadotte, the grandson of King Oscar II, was the president of the Swedish Red Cross during World War II and helped arrange for the prisoners' release. He also worked for the peaceful sur-render of German troops in Norway after the war. Folke Bernadotte was assassinated by a Jewish terrorist organization in Jerusalem in 1948, while mediating between Jews and Arabs.

Raoul Wallenberg, a Swedish diplomat, received much recognition for his Jewish rescue operation, in which Sweden granted asylum to thousands of Jews. In 1944, Wallenberg was appointed first secretary of the Swedish Legation in Budapest. Through his diplomacy, persuasive skills, and use of unconventional methods such as bribes and extortion, he became honored with saving at least a hundred thousand Jews. Raoul Wallenberg was eventually arrested by the Soviet Army and never heard from again.

In the 1950s and '60s Sweden spoke out against race discrimination in the United States and in the '70s against the United States' involvement in the Vietnam War. Because of its lack of military involvement, Sweden had great strength as an impartial judge. In the '70s, Sweden's prime minister, Olof Palme, proclaimed that neutrality does not mean isolation or indifference toward the world's problems.

THE GREAT DEPRESSION

World War I temporarily halted the growth of industrialism, and after the war Sweden underwent two economic recessions, one in 1921–2 and the other in 1929–33. Attention was focused on solving the country's problems, and being flexible and going with changing circumstances on the international market. The unemployment rate was high, and people lost their capital, their homes, and their savings. In 1932, almost one-third of industrial workers were unemployed.

In the years between the wars, Sweden held the belief that progress was still possible, and strove for greater equality among the people. With the institution of the law of universal suffrage, the social democrats became the largest party in the Riksdag. The Social Democratic Party's philosophy was influenced by Marxism, but modernized and adapted to Swedish thought and conditions. Later, welfare, or social democracy with the aim to transform society, became the preferred word,

Four generations of Swedes in 1932: the author's father, grandfather, great grandmother, and great great grandmother.

The author's great grandmother and father in the mid-1930s.

rather than socialism. Politics in modern Sweden have generally consisted of a five-way division of the parties: the conservatives, the liberals, the agrarians, the social democrats, and the communists. With the exception of a short break in 1936, the social democrats held power from 1932 to 1976.

In 1928, Per Albin Hanson, a social democrat who was later to become the prime minister, pushed for decreased unemployment and for a new reform of the welfare society, where people could live in privately owned houses or apartments in the suburbs to avoid overpopulation of central Stockholm. In the 1932 election, the social democrats received more votes than they had ever received in the past and returned to office. Many of their supporters were among the unemployed, and with the help of the votes from the Agricultural Party, the social democrats also won a majority in the Riksdag.

Despite the seriousness of unemployment and the agricultural crisis, technological development made it possible to increase the rate of building and construction. The social democrats suggested that the state use the unemployed workers to build roads and apartments, and that the workers be compensated with full salary. They reasoned that when people had money left over, they could increase their consumption of goods, which, in turn, would lead to industries hiring more workers. The social democrats were able to improve the situation through unemployment compensation and higher pensions. Not long thereafter, paid vacation was granted to everybody, along with better healthcare. The social democrats formed a strong government that would last for forty-four years. Many Swedes credit the social democrats with having the power of action, and with transforming Sweden from one of the poorer countries in Europe to one at the forefront of modern society.

By the late 1930s, the economy was on the upswing again, and people could afford to move into the newly built apartments. Note that Sweden has mostly apartment living around

The author's great grandmother and grandmother in the early 1930s

Apartment living in a typical modern suburb of Stockholm. Most of the apartments were built in the '50s and '60s in response to the rapid growth of the cities.

the big city areas. The idea of cooperative housing flourished, and tenants had a vested interest in many of these apartments, like those who own condominiums in the United States. Sweden recovered relatively quickly, and new businesses were soon growing. At the start of World War II, the standard of living had become one of the highest in the world.

During World War II, the push for social reform and the development of the welfare state were halted until after the war. But social problems, such as caring for the elderly and poor, were an issue. In 1945, Per Albin Hanson and his successor Tage Erlander (who became prime minister in 1946) again took the lead and pushed for nine-year mandatory education for all children and better care for the elderly, with the intent to lessen the gap between the social classes. In 1947, allowances for the unemployed, families with children, and retirees were instituted. The pension was raised enough to provide for almost all the needs of senior citizens, and later divided into general and occupational portions. In the 1950s the farming population saw a drastic drop—Sweden had achieved a high standard of living, and was working toward an urbanized welfare state.

CHANGES IN CRIMINAL CARE

The people of Sweden had for hundreds of years lived in poverty, struggling for their livelihood. Everybody was expected to do his or her part of the workload, and freeloaders, thieves, and other criminals were severely punished, often with death. For example, if a hungry person stole food from the more well off, the punishment might be death. A less severe penalty, for example, for an offender who had stolen a chicken was skamstocken (the log of shame). The accused had to stand tied to a log in the center of the market square or other public place and be ashamed of himself, while any passerby would hurl insults, spit, urinate, or throw rocks at him.

The death penalty was administered for what were considered more severe crimes, such as murder, witchcraft, incest, prostitution, maltreatment, and willful deceit. The last Swedish public execution took place in 1876, and the last in 1910, when a murderer by the name of Johan Alfred Andersson-Ander was sent to death by the guillotine. Imported from France, the guillotine was used in Sweden only this one time. Other more common ways to execute criminals were through hanging, firing squad, or handbila. Hanging was considered the most shameful way to die, reserved for thieves. Criminals were often hung on hilltops, where their bodies could easily be viewed from a distance away. In the unlikely event that the rope would break and the criminal didn't die on the first try, he was pardoned from the crime. The firing squad was normally reserved for military criminals. Handbila was a kind of beheading and considered the quickest, surest, and most honorable way to die. The criminal was blindfolded and tied to a tree log, and the head was severed from the body with a handheld axe. Sometimes the body was mutilated and cut into pieces that were tied to a wheel placed horizontally on top of a pole. This method was called stegling. The body was then left there to rot. In the hundred years between 1761 and 1860, 1063 people were executed in Sweden. Between the years 1861 and 1910, an additional 24 people were executed. The death penalty was abolished in 1921 for civilian crimes and in 1973 for military crimes.

In the twentieth century, Sweden adopted a more lenient philosophy of crime and punishment, although already around 1580, Olaus Petri said: " . . . *och straffet bör vara sådant, om möjligt är, att det icke förhindra honom, som straffad varder, till att bättra sig.*" (. . . and the punishment should be such, if it is possible, that it doesn't prevent him, who punished is, from bettering himself). The idea was to allow the criminal to rectify himself and become a better person, an idea with continued support in modern Sweden, where institutions for criminal care (or prisons) attempt to rehabilitate the criminal and send him back into society. Criminals are eligible for parole when they have served two-thirds of their sentence, and few of those sentenced to prison serve more than ten years. However, this system has achieved only moderate success. In the year 2000, 55 percent of parolees committed a second crime after their release.

WORLD WAR TWO

In the years between the wars, Sweden had cut back on its military and was lacking in adequate training both for winter operations and air raid defense. Before the outbreak of World War II, Swedish military preparedness was underdeveloped, and Sweden's readiness for a possible invasion was poor. However, need promotes the development of science and technology, and World War II was no different. Shortly after the outbreak of the war, more than three hundred thousand men were mobilized, trained, and placed in military posts along Sweden's coastlines. Eventually, nearly all men and thousands of women received training for the military or voluntary defense services.

Sweden declared, immediately after the start of the war, a position of neutrality, and was the only one of the Nordic countries to avoid direct conflict. Sweden had not been involved in a war since 1814; however, upholding a neutrality declaration in wartime proved difficult. Although Sweden had declared itself neutral, it also desired to keep its trade routes with other countries open and had to compromise on several accounts with Germany to avoid possible future conflicts. Germany was dependent on Swedish iron ore for its weapons industry, and Sweden fulfilled as much as 40 percent of Germany's needs. In addition, more than half of Sweden's imports came from Germany or from countries occupied by Germany. In order to meet its own needs for energy and food, Sweden continued trading with Germany, and Germany received

A family outing in 1939, at the start of World War II. Note the left hand traffic. Sweden switched to driving on the right side of the road in 1967.

much needed iron for the production of weapons. Those extensive exports of iron ore made critics question the validity of Sweden's neutrality declaration. Others called the export of iron ore a necessity, because it helped finance and support the Swedish population during the war, and thus prevented further involvement. Sweden also exported ball bearings to the United Kingdom.

In March 1940, the allies asked for permission to transport troops through Swedish territory on their way to assist Finland. Sweden declined for fear of German or Russian repercussions. In the spring of 1940, Germany invaded Denmark and Norway in an attempt to control Norwegian harbors that were important to the export of Swedish iron ore. The occupation of Norway cut off Sweden's trade routes with the Western world, forcing Sweden to ration its food and resources. Most of southern Sweden was also unprotected, and, in a still-controversial shift, Germany pressured Sweden into allowing military transports to go through the country on Swedish railroads.

Initially, Sweden refused to grant permission to the German transports of military equipment. Later, the agreement between neutral Sweden and Germany stipulated that the transports be of "humanitarian aid," such as medical equipment, food, and clothing, and still later, when Germany defeated Norway, of unarmed soldiers on leave. Between 1940 and 1943, more than 2 million German soldiers passed through Swedish territory. These concessions were, as much as possible, hidden from the public. When Germany started to weaken toward the end of the war, the allies reasoned that Sweden did not have much to fear and ought to help avoid prolonging the war. England continued trying to halt the export of iron ore to Germany, and in 1943, the transit of German personnel and weapons through Swedish territory was also halted.

Swedish children evacuated from the major cities to farms around the country during World War II.

During the Second World War, Sweden encouraged its people to be watchful of spies. In 1941, the "Swedish Tiger" became an important reminder. A man by the name of Bertil Almqvist drew the tiger, striped in the blue and yellow colors of the Swedish flag, and named it En Svensk Tiger, a pun that also means "A Swede Remains Silent." The Swedish Tiger became a symbol of Sweden as a watchful and silent nation, and was pictured on posters and on place mats in cafes to urge people not to blabber or answer a stranger's questions.

During both World Wars, Sweden made significant deviations from its neutrality declaration. Sweden has been heavily criticized for its support of Germany, including the sale of iron ore for weapons and permission of German military transport. Those who desire to study this issue further, for historical or philosophical reasons, might take into consideration, among other factors, Sweden's good relations with Germany through most of its history. It is also worth noting that during World War II most people, including Germany's own population, did not know of the horrors that went on at the Nazi death camps. That said, Swedish Nazi parties have never been represented at the *Riksdag*.

It is also important to examine to what extent a declaration of neutrality in a war zone is possible. Although the idea of true neutrality and the wish to stay out of conflict may be noble, it may also be naïve to think a country could stay neutral when surrounded by other nations at war. Total neutrality ends the moment one forms an opinion. Total neutrality would have meant a cutoff from international relations. Sweden, claiming non-participation in the wars, still suffered the effects of food and energy rationing.

Several other factors may also have affected the decision to allow the transports; for example, the possibility of a political crisis, along with King Gustav V's interest in allowing

German troops to pass through the country, which he explained in a statement regarding the danger of a possible German invasion (there are also suggestions that the king threatened to abdicate if the government couldn't agree on allowing the German transports). The fear of invasion, along with the more positive possibility of acquiring the Åland Islands with the help of Germany, might have tempted the Swedish politicians to waiver from their neutrality declaration. Later, as the winds shifted, Sweden also desired to come to the assistance of its Nordic brethren Norway, Finland, and Denmark.

THE MODERN MILITARY

Political and technological development in the twentieth century forced significant changes in the Swedish military. In 1901, the old system of the *indelningsverk* was abolished and Sweden instituted compulsory military service, consisting of a core group of professional soldiers and compulsory service for all men. The initial training period has been of varied length depending on the soldier's specialty, but usually between seven and a half and fifteen months, with several shorter periods of recurrent training throughout a man's life.

Prior to the outbreak of World War I, the Swedish military was prepared to meet an attack from Russia or Germany. Following the war, there was popular support for disarmament and, in 1925, the social democrats and the liberals pressured for military reduction and elimination of some of the outdated regiments. The Riksdag decided on cutbacks and modernization with the intent to stay elastic—to have the ability to strengthen the military if need be. The cavalry and reserve forces were abolished, the training time was shortened, and civilian service was permitted for conscientious objectors.

Sweden made its first military flight in 1912 and established its first flight squadron in the summer of that year. The air force was officially organized in 1925. Before the outbreak of World War II, industry flourished again. SAAB—Svenska Aeroplan Aktiebolaget (Swedish Aeroplane Incorporated) was founded in 1937, with the intent to build aircraft for the Swedish Air Force. Later, SAAB started manufacturing cars, too. SAAB has also been involved in the development of the modern fighter airplane JAS 39 Gripen. Their work on that plane started in the 1980s, after the air force had re-examined its equipment requirements and found a need to modernize. The JAS 39 Gripen fighter will have replaced most of the older fighters by the year 2006.

In the mid-1950s, threats of nuclear war led to a strong civilan defense, with the airforce developing into the fourth largest in the world. In 1968, another round of cutbacks started. The number of flight divisions was cut in half in the next decade. When several Russian submarines violated Swedish waters in the 1980s, and a Russian submarine ran aground in the Swedish Archipelago, Sweden was forced into greater vigilance and a re-examination of the country's defense policies.

In 1997, the military was again cut with the option to strengthen itself against possible invasions if need be. The experiences of the two world wars have led to the creation of "total defense," comprised of the military and civilian defense together, shaped to handle different types of threats and risks in peacetime as well as in times of war. The modern military is smaller than in the past, but well-trained and with the capacity to meet new threats and grow to full strength within one year. The military is comprised of three parts—the army, the navy, and the air force—that have different duties but the capacity to work together. Although the military of yesteryear was constructed to defend primarily against invasion, the modern military is more flexible and ready to adjust to different types of threats and needs, such as defending Sweden against armed attacks, maintaining territorial integrity, strengthening society during peacetime, and contributing to peace and safety in the rest of the world.

Military resources, both personnel and equipment, are employed to assist in accidents and natural catastrophes. The homeguard is comprised of fifty-eight thousand volunteers responsible for territorial defense, and for protecting buildings and projects against sabotage. The homeguard also plays a vital role in preparing society to handle peacetime problems, such as natural disasters, major accidents, and searches for missing persons.

A Royal Guard has existed at the palace in Stockholm since 1523 and is part of the security system. Until the middle of the nineteenth century, the guard was comprised of 100–200 men who were also trained firefighters. Later, when a regular police force was created, the Royal Guard was reduced to 30–50 men. Around 1960, the people who served in the Royal Guard were drawn from the whole country and all parts of the military (the army, the navy, the air force, and the homeguard). Today, approximately 70 soldiers stand guard around the clock at the Royal Palace, and another 45 at Drottningholms Slott, which is the royal family's primary residence. The ceremony of the changing of the guard takes about forty minutes and can be followed from Sergels Torg in the center of modern Stockholm to the Royal Palace in Old Town.

Presently, men are required to serve in the military at various times in their lives, from age eighteen to age forty-seven. Compulsory military service for women has been

Royal Guardsmen during the changing of the guard ceremony.
Photo: www.imagebank.sweden.se © Alexander V. Dokukin, Stockholm Visitors Board.

much debated in recent years. If the proposal passes, Sweden will be the second country in the world (after Israel) to require military service of women. But, unlike Israel, where compulsory military service for women is necessary to the nation's defense, in Sweden, it would be necessary to the equality of women. According to Folkpartiet (the People's Party) and the social democrats, the only way to achieve gender equality is by requiring military service of both men and women. The proposal is to test all men and women, and select the most fit of all citizens, not just of the male population. However, the results of a poll printed in *Aftonbladet* on March 6, 2000 revealed that the majority of women, 78 percent, did not want compulsory military service for themselves, while 81 percent felt it was okay to require it of men.

Chapter Ten
Welfare Age: 1950 to Present Day

THE WELFARE STATE

When World War II ended, Sweden was propelled into a new era of reform centered on Swedish democracy, founded on freedom of expression, freedom of opinion, and the observance of democratic processes, with the Riksdag its principal representative. The idea that all public power emanates from the people was emphasized and, in the 1950s, Sweden began to realize its goal of becoming a stable welfare state with work for everyone. The benefits of privileged groups were decreased for the benefit of the underprivileged. The weaker in society were to be provided for in health, housing, and jobs, with nobody left to fend for him or herself. The government was also responsible for the welfare of the country as a whole.

With the growth of the welfare state, true poverty and slums became extinct. The government provided financial aid for housing, and today Sweden has one of the highest standards of living and lowest rates of infant mortality in the world. Modern healthcare is of high quality. The public healthcare system charges only a nominal fee, or after an annual maximum has been spent, no fee at all. The most important points reached through the welfare state were basic social security for all, and an opportunity for individual growth through education.

Such benefits are costly and must be paid for through heavy taxation, which is not always to the people's liking.

Questions have been raised as to whether these sorts of governmental controls stifle individualism and initiative, and critics say the system causes high taxation and inflation. In addition, Swedish people are proponents of freedom of choice, and many feel that they live in a Big Brother society, where the government intrudes on their personal lives and deprives them of the chance to make their own choices. Not all are in favor of the small differences in pay between the highly educated people and those of lesser education. However, in general, the Swedish population supports the welfare state.

In 1953, paid vacation was increased to three weeks for all workers. In the '60s, paid vacation was increased to four weeks, and in the '70s to five weeks for everybody, regardless of where you worked. As more children were born and more women went to work outside of the home, daycare centers, *dag mammor* (day mothers, a municipality-employed nanny who keeps the child in her private home during normal working hours), and *fritidshem* (free-time homes, for after school activities) started to play bigger roles.

In the modern school system, sex education is taught from twelve years of age. Any religious subjects are general in nature; for example, general religious history and religions of the world are taught, but there is no particular emphasis on the Lutheran religion. The schools pride themselves on being friendly to children. The authoritarian mindset of the past does not exist any longer, and children call their teacher by first name or simply *fröken* (miss, for females), or *magistern* (schoolmaster, for males). Lunches and textbooks are free.

Mandatory school is nine years, plus one year of preschool. Secondary schools are two, three, or four years, and are free. Beneficial loans are available for those who need to support themselves while studying as adults. Specialization in music or sports is not taught in regular school. For example, general history of music is taught, but if you want to play the piano or the violin, you must do so on your own time. Likewise, general physical education is taught, but if you want to play a competitive team sport, such as hockey, you must join a hockey club after school hours. English is taught to everyone from third grade. German and French are the common choices for a second foreign language taught from seventh grade.

Public transportation is relatively inexpensive and easily available, especially in the big cities and suburbs, and most Swedes own only one car per family, which is used primarily when going on vacation or traveling to difficult-to-reach destinations. Subways and trains run on time and well into the night, and are kept clean and in good working condition. In most cities, the trains and subways leave so often (every few minutes) that you don't really need a timetable. A train/subway/bus card can be bought for the equivalent of about 80 American dollars a month. You can reach downtown Stockholm from most of the suburbs within twenty minutes, which makes public transportation a convenient and affordable way to commute.

After the abolishment of the bicameral parliament in 1971, the Riksdag reduced its 350 seats to 349 to avoid the possibility of a stalemate vote. In 1994, the election period changed from three to four years. In 1995, Sweden voted, with a small margin, to become a member of the European Union. Some consider this change to be the greatest threat yet to the democratic tradition that Sweden has struggled so long to achieve.

EQUALITY

Equality has been a hotly debated issue for most of the twentieth century, and much has been done to even the gaps between social classes as well as between men and women. Already in the 1970s, when the author went to grade school, both boys and girls learned the same subjects. For example, both boys and girls learned woodworking and sewing, cooking, home economics, and childcare.

Although reaching true equality is a long term and time-consuming goal, the focus was on eliminating class distinctions, and achieving equal pay, responsibilities, and benefits between men and women. People of status were no longer to be addressed by their title, but with the more casual *du* (you), or simply by first name.

An effort was also made in continuing education for the adult population. Women were encouraged to go out and *förverkliga sig* (seek self-actualization), to seek education, and to enter the more technical or male-dominated workforce. The traditional society, with men working outside of the home and women tending to the home and children, was viewed as an oppressive situation for the female population. But, in many people's opinion, the work for equality still fell short. For example, women felt that by joining the workforce, they only added more work to their many responsibilities to home and family. They felt that although they worked outside of the home as many hours as their husbands did, their husbands did not share equally in the household duties. In addition, many of the women would rather have stayed at home while the children were small, but high taxes made it difficult for a family to survive on only one person's income. The housewife was at a disadvantage both in economic terms (for example, in building a pension) and in terms of equality (for example, in the way she was viewed by society).

Sweden has one of the highest divorce rates in the world, and fewer Swedes get married today than ever before. A full 44 percent of all children are born to unmarried couples. However, being born to unmarried parents does not necessarily suggest that the mother alone raises the children. Couples still live together as husband and wife, but without the official marriage license.

At the start of the twenty-first century, an even greater effort was made to even the gap between men and women; for example, by suggesting compulsory military service for women, and by introducing paid *barn ledighet* (childcare leave) for fathers. In the past, women received nine months paid maternity leave. Today, the mother and father of the new child receive 480 days (approximately sixteen months) paid leave together, and 60 days are reserved for each parent. The rest can be divided as the parents see fit. The father also has the right to 10 days leave in conjunction with the birth of the baby. According to Statistiska Centralbyrån (Central Bureau of Statistics), in the year 1999–2000, the average new parents split their leave with mothers staying at home 87.8 percent of the time and fathers 12.2 percent. In general, couples still choose the traditional roles.

Jämställdhet (equality) is a beautiful word, but a difficult one to live by. Still, Sweden has a reputation as a country with greater gender equality than any other nation. In general, the male population supports, seeks out, and accepts equality and women's liberation from the traditional mindset. Sweden's greatest rock poet, Ulf Lundell, expresses in one of his songs (after having traveled to Berlin and Paris, and to New York and Key West) his longing to be (together) with a "Stockholmgal" again:

> *... och hålla en hand som är stark ... och kyssa en kvinna som är vuxen och fri, som står stadigt på medveten mark ... jag vill va med en Stockholmstjej igen ...* (... and hold a hand that is strong ... and kiss a woman who is grown-up and free, who stands steady on well-known ground ... I want to be with a Stockholmgal again ...)

—Ulf Lundell

LABOR MARKET AND INDUSTRY

The years following World War II were the golden age of Swedish industry. The biggest companies, such as SAAB, Volvo, ASEA, L.M. Ericsson, and Electrolux gave employment to thousands and also sold their products abroad.

The growth of production and rapid expansion of industry in the '50s and '60s helped increase the standard of living. In the 1960s, Sweden saw a stable economy and low unemployment, where immigrants could easily find jobs. In fact, after the war, Sweden was in such need of labor that it accepted immigrants in large numbers from many different countries to fill job vacancies. However, the refugees that came to Sweden from Turkey, Chile, or Czechoslovakia seldom learned to speak the language (with the exception of the children), in general did not mingle with the Swedes or try to fit in, and were therefore not as readily accepted into Swedish society as the immigrants who had come, for example, from Greece to fill job vacancies.

Sweden made the effort to provide ethnic, linguistic, and religious minorities with the right to preserve their traditional social lives, and to provide native language training for the children of immigrants. But the downside of this was that it also gave immigrant children the extra burden of being branded as outsiders by their peers. Sweden'sgood intentions often did not translate into the open and welcoming society that they hoped for. Approximately 11 percent of Sweden's population is first generation immigrants.

From the middle of the 1960s, greater competition on the international market and inflation affected domestic politics, and production stagnated. In the late '70s and early '80s, the market changed drastically, and the improvement in living standards slowed. The oil crisis of the mid-'70s contributed to higher prices on products, and many companies had to shut their doors. The shipbuilding and mining industries became dependent on industrial politics, which focused on helping businesses survive the tougher times. But the drawback was a slowing of the transformation of the industry toward higher productivity. In an attempt to strengthen the export industry and become more competitive abroad, the Swedish crown was devalued three times in the 1970s. Waves of refugees also arrived, but failed to find employment.

Sweden was forced to adapt to the fact that similar goods could be manufactured for lower prices in other countries. The quick development of the international market, specifically larger industrialized companies, forced many smaller companies to expand their organizations if they were to survive. Swedish industry in the 1980s was comprised of less expensive export goods, with new technology for production and communications which opened up new opportunities. For example, the Swedish steel industry has changed from producing goods in high quantity to producing specialized products, such as stainless steel and precision tools. The car industry has shifted toward producing expensive and more prestigious cars. New discoveries have been made in telecommunications and pharmaceutical products.

In the early '90s, unemployment rose to nearly 9 percent, and nearly 40 percent of the industrial workers were laid off. Although new businesses were established, Swedish industry was decreased by 25 percent. Following the crisis came a strong focus on bettering the efficiency in industry. Today, there is more production than in the last decade, despite the smaller number of workers. In March 2004, unemployment had stabilized to 5.8 percent.

DEMAND FOR ENERGY

In the early '60s, more electric power was produced, but Sweden could not keep up with the great demands for energy, and waterpower only supplied the country with one-fifth of its need. Oil was in particularly great demand, which made Sweden dependent on the import of energy sources. The economic crisis and high unemployment in the '70s resulted in part from dramatic hikes in oil prices.

To avoid the uncertainties of the oil market, Sweden decided to supplement hydroelectric power with nuclear power. Nuclear power was a hope for Sweden's future energy problems and gave the country the possibility of becoming energy independent. But dissatisfaction over high taxes, the unstable economy, and the danger of nuclear power caused concerns and political controversies. This issue became crucial in the 1976 election.

After an intense campaign about nuclear power, the non-socialist block won the election. This success came after forty-four years of socialist government. The power shifted from the social democratic/communist coalition to the moderate/liberal/center coalition, but was only to last for a few years. The Social Democratic Party was still the largest single party in the Riksdag.

A referendum in 1980 stated that nuclear power was to be phased out. However, the great majority of voters favored continuation of the nuclear power plants already in existence for the duration of their operating life. The Riksdag therefore decided to phase out the plants by the year 2010. Later, the plan was decided to be economically impossible.

The issue of nuclear energy attracted a great deal of public attention, and the Chernobyl accident in 1986 only reinforced the belief that the reactors had to be shut down. Sweden was heavily affected by the accident: thousands of reindeer had to be destroyed, and eating wild berries and mushrooms was banned for a decade to come. Today, Sweden has eleven nuclear reactors (in addition to one that has been prematurely shut down), from which the country gets about half of its energy, with the remaining energy coming from hydroelectric power and a small percentage from fossil fuels.

In general, in the last decade public opinion has been positive toward nuclear energy. In 1996, a survey conducted by the Confederation of Swedish Industries found 80 percent of those surveyed in favor of nuclear energy, and against premature closures of the plants, especially if it increased fossil fuel use. A poll in 2003 indicated that 74 percent of the people felt that environmental priority and restraining greenhouse gas emissions were of utmost concern, and only 14 percent favored a nuclear phase-out.

Most Swedes are conscious of the environment, and many feel that nuclear power is gentler toward the environment than coal, gas, and oil. The proponents of nuclear energy feel that it would be a mistake of great proportions, regarding environmental protection and the nation's economy, to turn away from nuclear power.

OLOF PALME

From the 1930s onward, the Social Democratic Party has held the dominant position in the Riksdag. In 1969, Olof Palme became the new prime minister. Palme is noted for introducing the unicameral parliament in 1971, for making the monarch a pure ceremonial head of state, and for changing the order of succession, giving women an equal right to inheritance of the crown. Therefore, the firstborn princess Victoria will become the queen of Sweden when the current king, Carl XVI Gustaf, passes on (note the different spelling of the name, Carl Gustaf, instead of Karl Gustav of earlier generations). The defenders of social democracy consider Olof Palme one of the great heroes of the world and an outspoken advocate of disarmament, who worked for justice, equality, and world peace.

Olof Palme was raised in an upper middle class home, but strove for all of his life to establish equality, peace, and social justice. Palme was committed from his early youth to human solidarity, especially regarding the oppressed peoples of the world. He became a dynamic leader in social and economic democracy and equality.

Through Palme's work to build a society based on security for all, the pension system was improved, schools and daycare centers were expanded, and all people were given the opportunity for an education. The basic idea was that those with power were obligated to work for the welfare of the people. The Swedish welfare state experienced its greatest expansion during Palme's leadership. In addition, Palme stressed that a strong and free Sweden had an obligation to contribute to a better world. He worked for basic moral issues and legitimate human rights. For example, he stressed that democratic socialists should struggle against oppression, and work to unite and liberate people who were denied political and human rights. He was a proponent of disarmament and protested against the United States' involvement in the Vietnam War. He sympathized with the Palestinians, accepted political refugees, and worked tirelessly to liberate third world countries from oppression. He consistently demonstrated his solidarity toward the oppressed peoples of the world, and presented a constant challenge to the Western world on issues that obstructed international action. He strove to educate the people in order that he might obtain their support, and in the hope that others would follow his example.

In 1986, Sweden received one of its biggest blows ever, which caught the people unprepared and came as a shock to

This plaque, mounted in the sidewalk at the murder site, is a monument to Olof Palme, and reads: "Sweden's Prime Minister, Olof Palme, was murdered here on the 28th of February, 1986."

much of the rest of the world. Prime Minister Olof Palme was shot and killed on a sidewalk in central Stockholm while walking home with his wife from the movie theater (Swedish politicians are in the habit of mingling with the people and using public transportation, without the company of an entourage of security guards.) The motive of the killer is still unknown.

The outspoken, committed, energetic, and accomplished Palme had often stirred controversy on the political circuit.

NK, Nordiska Kompaniet, the large department store in Stockholm where Anna Lindh, Minister of Foreign Affairs, was murdered by a knife-wielding assailant in September 2003.
Photo: www.imagebank.sweden.se © Richard Ryan, Stockholm Visitors Board.

But even the non-socialist population felt a kind of love-hate for him, and spoke of his assassination as the day Sweden lost its innocence and joined in the ranks of crime and brutality. Palme's murder came after the country had been spared from political violence for nearly two hundred years. Sweden went into mourning. Today, almost twenty years later, you can still find red roses (the Social Democratic Party's symbol) on the sidewalk at the murder site.

Olof Palme was an important political figure worldwide, and it is safe to say that he was modern Sweden's most important political figure. He is remembered for his significant contributions to human rights and foreign affairs issues. After Palme's assassination, Mr. Oliver Tambo, president of the African National Congress of South Africa, described him as, "an international statesman . . . one of us . . . who has made an inestimable contribution to the struggle of the liberation of South Africa . . . a giant of justice who had become a citizen of the world . . ."

Chapter Eleven
Traditions and Culture from Ancient to Modern

NORRLAND

We have spent considerable time on the events and people of the more densely populated middle and southern Sweden. However, it is in place to devote at least a small section to Norrland or Lapland, the northernmost two-thirds of the country. Norrland is sparsely populated, with few towns, and characterized by powerful rivers, midnight sun, and northern lights. Large areas of Norrland are designated for reindeer herding, and only 10 percent of the country's population, including the Sami (Laps), live there.

Lapland is the name of a region overlapping several countries. The Sami, the indigenous people of northern Scandinavia, are traditionally known as a nomadic reindeer-herding people who have the Scandinavian peninsula since four thousand years ago. The Sami live in the area stretching from northern Norway, Sweden, and Finland to the Russian Kola peninsula. There are approximately seventeen thousand Swedish Sami. It is believed that the Sami followed herds of reindeer to the area after the last Ice Age. Rock carvings, some as old as five thousand years, testify to the age of Sami culture. Because of the widespread area the Sami occupy, the Sami can be thought of in terms of a way of life, rather than in terms of a

Swift rivers and sparsely populated areas of land are some of the signs of the north.

specific race of people. The name Sami has its origin in *Suomi* (the Finnish name for Finland), which originally stems from Sämä, and refers to the area north of the Gulf of Finland.

For thousands of years, the Sami lived more or less disconnected from the rest of Europe. However, tales suggest long lasting conflicts with the Vikings and also trade with travelers from northern Europe. In the 1500s, the Swedish king Gustav Vasa declared that, "all permanently uninhabited land belongs to God, us, and the Swedish crown." By that, he meant also the land occupied by the Sami. Since the Sami were a nomadic people, their land did not qualify as permanently inhabited.

This declaration led to colonization attempts of the north, and the native Sami lost large areas of land. Later, several tries were made to convert the Sami to Christianity, and the Sami were forbidden to speak their native language. The languages of the Sami have their origin in Finnish, Estonian, and Hungarian, and are divided into three main dialects that are so different from each other that they could really be called three Sami languages. These languages are further broken down into nine sub-dialects.

The Sami are a cultural minority, not unlike the American Indian, who elect a representative assembly with limited power to distribute their funds. Their economy is based mainly on farming, hunting, and handicraft. Today, the Sami people are recognized as one of the oldest surviving minority cultures of the world.

Since the mid-1900s, most Sami have settled in towns and villages. In an attempt to promote cooperation between the Sami, the Nordic Sami Council was established in 1956. The Sami Council has been recognized as a legitimate spokesman for the Sami people and recommended that: "The policy of the national state must be to give the Sami-speaking population the opportunity to preserve its language and other cultural customs on terms that accord with the expressed wishes of the Sami themselves." As a result, it is possible for Sami children to speak their language in school, and even complete university degrees in their native tongue.

CULTURE AND LEISURE

Most of us are familiar with such famous artists as August Strindberg, Sweden's greatest writer of drama and fiction, and such movie giants as director Ingmar Bergman and actor Max von Sydow. And most of us have heard of ABBA. But fewer people outside of Sweden are as familiar with, or understand, such beloved artists as Carl Larsson (painter), Evert Taube (troubadour), Povel Ramel (composer/singer/actor/comedian), Lasse Åberg (actor/comedian/painter), and Cornelis Vreeswijk (singer/troubadour).

Carl Larsson is best known for his paintings of happy, and very Swedish, family life, mostly picturing children around the turn of the twentieth century. Evert Taube wrote many songs about life at sea, often depicting a fictional sailor, Fritiof Andersson, and later a family man, Rönnerdal. His lyrics describe his love of the simple and beautiful relations with peoples of the world, and have become poetry with which the Swedish population can easily identify. Povel Ramel has written more than eight hundred songs. He became famous for his parodies, with their clever lyrics. Lasse Åberg acted in several children's programs and family comedies, and also designed the seat covers that are in use today on the subways in Stockholm. Cornelis Vreeswijk was born in the Netherlands in 1937, but lived in Sweden from 1949 to his death in 1987. His songs, often siding with society's poor and outcast, used modern language but bridged into history.

Somliga går med trasiga skor, säg vad beror det på? (Some of us walk in worn-out shoes, say, why is this so?)

—Cornelis Vreeswijk

Although Cornelis Vreeswijk was foreign born, the Swedish people still regard him as one of their own. Vreeswijk lived in Sweden for most of his life, died in Sweden, and is buried at Katarina Kyrkogård in Stockholm. He spoke perfect Swedish without any hint of an accent, and he understood the Swedish mindset.

The Concert Hall in Stockholm, with the fountain Orfeus, *by the artist Carl Milles.*

For leisure, many Swedes spend their summers in a *sommarstuga* (summer cottage), often a red cottage by the water. About one-fifth of all Swedish families own a summer home in the country. A great deal of money is also spent on holidays and travel throughout Europe. For those who vacation in the winter, the sunny Canary Islands are a popular travel destination, as well as many other European countries. Much time is also spent in nature or sailing Skärgården (the Archipelago; the waters outside of Stockholm are speckled with islands). Because of Allemansrätten (all man's right, a general right to public access), which is unique to Sweden and the Scandinavian countries, Swedish people have access to nature and all areas of non-cultivated land. For example, as long as you avoid destructive practices, you can pick berries or flowers and swim in lakes without asking permission, paying a fee, or requiring a lifeguard. So called "national parks" do not exist, as all of nature is treated as one. You can even camp out wherever you please, as long as you are not directly in somebody's back yard. The idea is that all people have the right to use all of the land for their personal enjoyment and leisure.

TRADITION AND HOLIDAYS

People's need for togetherness, feast, and celebration leads to a shared happiness. Most of us are familiar with New Year's Eve and the Easter and Christmas holidays (Swedish people celebrate Christmas Eve rather than Christmas Day), so this section will focus mostly on the history of those holidays and traditions that are typically Swedish: Valborg, Midsommar, Advent, and Lucia. Many Swedish holidays and traditions are based on religious *sagor* (stories) and myth stemming from Swedish heathen and Catholic times. Many

216

Swedish cottage by the water in the 1930s.

The sommarstuga *where the author spent summers as a child. This cottage is approximately 150 years old.*

people continue celebrating, but are unaware of the real reasons behind these holidays.

Valborg, on April 30, celebrates the coming of spring through the lighting of huge fires. For several months prior to the holiday, people collect twigs, wood, and other items that can be burned, and build a huge pile, normally in the middle of a field designated for this tradition. When the pile is finally set on fire, it has usually grown to several meters in height and ten to fifteen meters across. Students, both those who graduated decades ago and those who are about to graduate that spring, dress in their white *studentmössor* (student caps). Few people still note that Valborg is celebrated in the memory of the German saint Walburg, who lived around AD 700. It is theorized that the fires were originally lit in connection with letting the cattle out on the fields at the coming of spring. Wolf and bear were common all the way down into southern Sweden until the mid-1700s, and the fires were lit in the hope that they would frighten the wild animals away from the cattle.

Midsommar (midsummer) is, together with Christmas, considered the most important traditional holiday and is celebrated around the summer solstice. Women bind flower garlands for themselves and their daughters to wear in their hair. Whatever wildflowers one can find locally on the fields and in the forests are used, often in the colors of white, pink, blue, and yellow; for example, *prästkrage* (daisy), *klöver* (clover), *blåklint* (cornflower), and *lejongap* (snapdragon). A *midsommarstång* (midsummer pole, sometimes called a maypole) is dressed in leaves. Both adults and children dance and play games around the pole. There are also competitions in the Swedish folk dances, such as polka, hambo, and schottis.

Note: The word *majstång* (maypole) has nothing to do with the month of May. The word *maj* means "green twig." Midsummer is celebrated around the summer solstice in the end

*The author, ten years old, dancing around
the midsummer pole in the summer of 1974.*

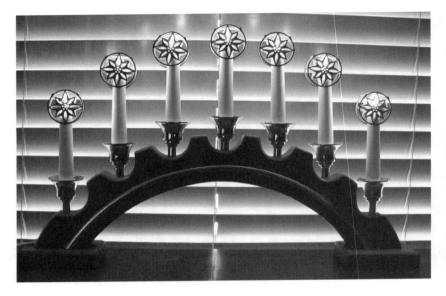

Seven-armed electric candleholder popular in Sweden during Advent.

of June, and to *maja en stång* (may a pole) is old Swedish, meaning to dress the pole in green leaves in a way to express gratitude that spring and summer have finally come.

Advent means arrival (the arrival of Jesus Christ) and starts with the first Sunday in December. A candleholder is decorated with moss and red berries, and the first candle of four is lit. One more candle is lit each successive Sunday. *Adventsstjärnor* (electrical Advent stars) are hung in the windows, and the seven-armed electric candleholder is placed in the window and lit. In December, sunrise occurs around 8:30 A.M. in the Stockholm area. When the author started school in the early '70s, each child was allowed to keep a lit candle on his or her desk in the morning, in a homemade clay candleholder, while the teacher read stories from the Bible.

Lucia, or Saint Lucia, is the festival of light and is celebrated on December 13 as a preliminary to Christmas. The name Lucia stems from the Latin prefix *luci-*, meaning light. But the legend of young Saint Lucia, who was executed because of her Christian beliefs on this day around the year AD 300, comes from Sicily. Saint Lucia comes with light in a time when we need it the most. The Lucia tradition brings an atmosphere of song and of hope for spring's return. Children get up early and serve *lussekatter* (a sweet bread containing raisins and saffron) to their mothers and fathers.

> *Mörkret skall flykta snart ur jordens dalar . . . Dagen skall åter ny, stiga ur rosig sky . . . Sancta Lucia, Sancta Lucia . . .* (Darkness shall soon flee the world's valleys. . . Daylight shall once again, rise from a rosy sky . . . Saint Lucia, Saint Lucia . . .)

—from the Italian Saint Lucia
song. The Swedish text
was written by Arvid Rosen
in 1928.

Afterword

PUBLIC POWER OF THE PEOPLE

Sweden was one of the last regions to emerge from under the ice sheet that covered Europe more than ten thousand years ago. Modern Sweden is a prosperous industrial nation with a small population of approximately 9 million people. Despite its relatively large surface area, Sweden is one of the most sparsely populated countries in Europe. Forests of pine, spruce, and birch trees, along with mountains in the north and thousands of lakes, cover more than half of the country. In modern Sweden, only about 10 percent of the country is covered by farmland, mainly around Skåne in the most southern part.

In combination with the private sector, the Swedish government influences the development of the economy. The Swedish welfare state has reached great achievements in standard of living, economic security, and class and gender equality. But with all its good intentions, the system is still far from perfect. There is a lot of grumbling about social issues and, yes, still a lot of grumbling about taxes. The situation often reminds me of the saying about having your cake and eating it, too. The Swedes want to retain all the benefits of the social welfare program, but would rather do without *socialism*. This would certainly be difficult. Many people have also become dissatisfied with the labor unions feeling the unions, have self-serving motives and have lost touch with

223

the real problems of the workers. The Swedish people are always on the lookout for possible abuse of authority.

Throughout the writing of this book, I have tried to stick strictly with facts, as a historian should, without expressing personal or moral opinion. However, it has been difficult to avoid the temptation to let my passions shine through. I have looked at the cycles of war and rebellion, and thought about what it is that triggers the pattern to continue: the pursuit of power by a select few at the expense of the common man. It is my belief that the struggle against oppression is the driving force behind the development of the social welfare state and the idea that, in a prosperous nation, the power must reside with the people.

As a native of Sweden, I have found the journey from Ice Age to modern day intriguing and far-reaching. Twenty-five years after finishing high school, I finally feel that I understand the importance of the street names in my hometown, Jakobsberg, just outside of Stockholm: Folkungavägen, Engelbrektsvägen, Frihetsvägen, Margaretavägen, Dackevägen, Vasavägen, Allmogeplatsen . . . they all speak of the people and events that have, for hundreds of years, stood behind the building of the democratic, industrialized, and modern welfare state that Sweden is today.

Index

Other Illustrated Histories
from Hippocrene...

The Arab World: An Illustrated History *(Kirk Sowell)*
293 pages • 50 photos/maps/illus. • 5½ X 8½ • 0-7818-0990-8 • (465) • $14.95pb

Arizona: An Illustrated History *(Patrick Lavin)*
252 pages • 60 photos/maps/illus. • 5 X 7 • 0-7818-0852-9 • (102) • $14.95pb

California: An Illustrated History *(Robert Chandler)*
252 pages •60 photos/maps/illus • 5½ X 8½ • 0-7818-0990-8 • (583) • $14.95pb

The Celtic World: An Illustrated History *(Patrick Lavin)*
185 pages • 50 photos/maps/illus. • 5 X 7 • 0-7818-0731-X • (582) • $14.95hc

China: An Illustrated History *(Yong Ho)*
142 pages • 50 photos/maps/illus. • 5 X 7 • 0-7818-0821-9 • (154) • $14.95hc

Cracow: An Illustrated History *(Zdzisław Zygulski)*
160 pages • 60 photos/maps/illus. • 5 X 7 • 0-7818-0837-5 • (542) • $12.95pb

England: An Illustrated History *(Henry Weisser)*
166 pages • 50 photos/maps/illus. • 5 X 7 • 0-7818-0751-4 • (446) • $11.95hc

Florida: An Illustrated History *(Robert A. Taylor)*
223 pages • 50 photos/maps/illus. • 5½ X 8½ • 0-7818-1052-3 • (36) • $14.95hc

France: An Illustrated History *(Lisa Neal)*
214 pages • 55 photos/maps/illus. • 5 X 7 • 0-7818-0872-3 • (340) • $12.95pb

Greece: An Illustrated History *(Tom Stone)*
181 pages • 50 photos/maps/illus. • 5 X 7 • 0-7818-0755-7 • (557) • $14.95hc

Ireland: An Illustrated History *(Henry Weisser)*
166 pages • 50 photos/maps/illus. • 5 X 7 • 0-7818-0693-3 • (782) • $11.95hc

Israel: An Illustrated History *(David C. Gross)*
160 pages • 50 photos/maps/illus. • 5 X 7 • 0-7818-0756-5 • (024) • $11.95hc

Italy: An Illustrated History *(Joseph Privitera)*
142 pages • 50 photos/maps/illus. • 5 X 7 • 0-7818-0819-7 • (436) • $14.95hc

Japan: An Illustrated History *(Shelton Woods)*
200 pages • 50 photos/maps/illus.• 5 X 7 • 0-7818-0989-4 • (469) • $14.95pb

Korea: An Illustrated History *(David Rees)*
147 pages • 50 photos/maps/illus. • 5 X 7 • 0-7818-0873-1 • (354) • $12.95pb

Mexico: An Illustrated History *(Michael Burke)*
183 pages • 50 photos/maps/illus. • 5 X 7 • 0-7818-0690-9 • (585) • $11.95hc

Paris: An Illustrated History *(Elaine Mokhtefi)*
150 pages • 50 photos/maps/illus. • 5 X 7 • 0-7818-0838-3 • (136) • $12.95pb

Poland: An Illustrated History *(Iwo C. Pogonowski)*
270 pages • 50 photos/maps/illus. • 5 X 7 • 0-7818-0757-3 • (404) • $14.95hc

Poland in WWII: An Illustrated Military History *(Andrew Hempel)*
114 pages • 50 photos/maps/illus. • 5 X 7 • 0-7818-0758-1 • (541) • $11.95hc

Russia: An Illustrated History *(Joel Carmichael)*
252 pages • 50 photos/maps/illus. • 5 X 7 • 0-7818-0689-5 • (154) • $14.95hc

Spain: An Illustrated History *(Fred James Hill)*
175 pages • 50 photos/maps/illus. • 5 X 7 • 0-7818-0874-X • (339) • $12.95pb

Tikal: An Illustrated History of the Ancient Maya Capital
(John Montgomery)
271 pages • 80 photos/maps/illus. • 6 X 9 • 0-7818-0853-7 • (101) • $14.95pb

Prices subject to change without notice. **To purchase Hippocrene Books** contact your local bookstore, call (718) 454-2366, or write to: HIPPOCRENE BOOKS, 171 Madison Avenue, New York, NY 10016. Please enclose check or money order, adding $5.00 shipping (UPS) for the first book and $.50 for each additional book.